A Good Word for Jesus

A Heretic's Testimony

by

Paul Trudinger

OPEN GATE PRESS
incorporating Centaur Press
LONDON

First published in 2007 by Open Gate Press
51 Achilles Road, London NW6 1DZ

Copyright © 2007 by Paul Trudinger
All rights, by all media, reserved.

British Library Cataloguing-in-Publication Programme
A catalogue record for this book is available from the British Library.

ISBN 978 1 871871 64 7

Cover illustration: The Prophets fresco in the Salle de la Grande Audience, detail depicting the Prophets Moses and Isaiah, c.1344-5, Giovanetti, Matteo / Palais des Papes, Avignon / The Bridgeman Art Library

The author would like to thank Desmond O'Keeffe, editor of *The Downside Review*, for permission to reproduce the article in Appendix A on pp. 82-85.

The author would also like to thank Keith Gilley, editor of *Faith and Freedom*, for permission to reproduce the article in Appendix B on pp. 86-101.

Printed and bound in Great Britain by
Antony Rowe Limited, Chippenham, Wiltshire

Contents

Dedicatory Acknowledgements iv

Chapter 1	" ... A Good Word for Jesus"	7
Chapter 2	Who Needs Jesus?	14
Chapter 3	Was Jesus *the* Christ?	24
Chapter 4	Jesus and *the* Resurrection	34
Chapter 5	More, more, about Jesus	45
Chapter 6	St. Paul, the Damascus Road, "My Gospel", and Jesus	54
Chapter 7	With Respect To 'God'	62
Chapter 8	Tying up some Loose Ends: Concerning Prayer – Life after Death – With Regard to the Bible	74
Appendix A	'"I know that my Redeemer liveth" A Note on *Job* 19: vv. 25 & 26'	82
Appendix B	'The Gospels as Pauline Christology historicized – A Speculation revisited'	86
Endnotes		102
Index		107

Dedicatory Acknowledgements

There have been many people who, over the years, have influenced my thinking which has led to the conclusions set forth in this book. In some instances this influence has been unbeknownst to the persons here cited. I have been stimulated as much by those who have disagreed with these conclusions as by those who have indicated general agreement. I wish to acknowledge the influence of at least *some* of these folk by dedicating this small book to:

John and Mavis Bodycomb
(see Chapter 2)

Desmond Davey, Garnet Hills,
Gordon MacDermid, and Eleanor Stebner
(erstwhile colleagues)

Stefan Jonasson, Fr. Wayne Morissey,
Fr. Ronald McCullough and Peter Friend
(conversation partners over many years)

Bruce Martin
(the good physician)

Brian Hern
(the beloved accountant)

Graeme Pitt
(honest, questing pastor)

David Forward
(who first alerted me to the 'heresies' of Albert Schweitzer)

Tom Atherton
(most helpful positive critic)

Byron and Robin
(a most serendipitous meeting)

Margaret and John

And in memory of dear Ricky

A Good Word for Jesus

CHAPTER 1
" ... A Good Word for Jesus"

In his book, *Beside the Bonnie Brier Bush,* Ian MacLaren writes of an elderly Scottish mother who on her death bed said to her son, "Remember! Always speak a good word for Jesus."[1] Although not addressed, of course, to me, I have always followed her request and I believe I can truthfully say that I have never made a derogatory remark or statement about Jesus. I have to admit that there have been times in conversations in a group or in one-to-one encounters when I perhaps could have spoken about my commitment to follow Jesus but have refrained from doing so. When the subject of Jesus has ever arisen in my presence, however, I have spoken about his influence in my life, unashamedly. His life, his words and deeds have guided me on countless occasions. If I were asked how this commitment came about, I would say that it was largely because I was brought up by devout parents and Jesus held a high place in our home's conversations. His example of compassion for the outcasts of society amongst whom he seemed quite at home, has always attracted me to him. I want to follow in his way.

My parents were conservative Christian medical missionaries who believed that Jesus was God's very self in our midst. This, for them, and for me as a child, accounted for his recorded ability to turn water into wine, to walk on water, and to feed five thousand people with five loaves and two fishes. Such miraculous 'nature-defying' deeds, even if they were actually historical, which I believe they were not, would somewhat diminish Jesus' stature for me. I do believe such stories can have important symbolical meaning. I do not believe, however, that Jesus was God, and I have strong reasons for believing that he was not "*The* Christ", "he that should come". I will outline these reasons in Chapter 3.

Many non-Christians are similarly attracted to the Jesus I follow. When the American Methodist missionary, E. Stanley Jones, arrived in India, he asked Mahatma Gandhi what he (Jones) should best do to help the Indian people. Gandhi replied, "Be like Jesus." A leading North American Sufi, Murat Yagan, (Sufism is a strong branch of Islamic spiritualism), came to conduct a seminar in Winnipeg where I was teaching. Amongst other inspiring things he said, he stated that if he had to name the person in human history who was *for him* the best exponent of what he called "a lightning rod" – bringing God's power and purpose into our midst, he would say "Jesus". The great twentieth-century Jewish philosopher, Martin Buber, wrote of Jesus' importance to him, calling him one of his most significant 'elder brothers'.[2]

Most orthodox Christians would say that these "good words spoken for Jesus" by the above three non-Christians are not nearly enough. They believe that Jesus was sent to earth by God to be the one who by his *death*, even more than by his life and teaching, would make an altogether sufficient and efficacious sacrifice to atone for the sins of the whole world, thus enabling all who trust in him to embrace God's salvation. I understand this viewpoint; I was brought up to believe it and for many years I taught and preached it

CHAPTER 1

wholeheartedly. I now no longer can agree with it as being the truth about Jesus and this for reasons of conscience and honesty with regard to evidence, quite a bit of it Scriptural evidence. Martin Luther is reported as having written, "My conscience is under bondage to Holy Scripture, and it is always wrong to go against conscience".[3] He did not say "it is always wrong to go against Scripture." His conscience in that context was "under bondage" to a particular portion of Scripture: Paul's Epistle to the Romans. My conscience, likewise, is compelled by the evidence of certain passages of Scripture, both in the Old and New Testaments, to reject the orthodox teaching summarised above as not being true to the historical person and teaching of Jesus. It came about, and for understandable reasons, as part of the development of early followers of Jesus and in particular, I believe, the development of Paul's thinking. I will write much more about this in later chapters.

Christians call Jesus the "Saviour", but that is a term belonging (in its universal capital 'S' sense) to God alone. Jesus' very name, *Jehoshua* (Yeshu or Joshua) *means* Yahweh (God) saves". It was the celebration, as the Hebrew people believed it to be, of God's liberating act in guiding the children of Israel into the Promised Land under the leadership of Moses' successor, Joshua, which gave the sixth book of the Bible the title, the Book of Joshua. The Greek Old Testament calls it the Book of *Jesus*. I feel sure that Jesus would have heartily endorsed the words of the Psalmist: "God is my light and my *salvation*; whom then shall I fear?" Most Christians, even amongst those who do not readily accept many of the Church's credal statements, still feel the need to assert that Jesus was *the* clearest, the most compelling demonstration in human history of God's nature and intention for humankind. I very much doubt that Jesus himself would be happy to have that said about him, presuming that he is alive in the Spirit world, which I believe he is. I feel confident that if one had asked, during his ministry, whether what he was teaching and practising went beyond the words of Micah the prophet (Ch. 6: 8), "What does Yahweh require of you but that you do justice, love mercy, and walk humbly with your God?" Jesus would have answered something like, "Goodness me, no; that is the heart of my message and my practice of faith." One major contemporary writer about Jesus, Marcus Borg, in a brief article "What did Jesus know?",[4] states that above all Jesus *knew* God. Yet again I would suggest that were we to have asked Jesus, "Do you know God in an essentially deeper way than the Psalmist who wrote

> O Lord, thou hast searched me and known me.
> ... thou understandest my thought afar off.
> ... and art acquainted with all my ways ...
> Thou hast beset me behind and before,
>   and laid thine hand upon me ...
> Whither shall I go from thy spirit? or whither
>   shall I flee from thy presence?
> If I ascend up into heaven, thou art there: if I
> make my bed in hell, behold, thou art there ... ?"
>
> (*Psalm* 139: 1-3, 5, 7-8,
> Authorised Version),

I am convinced that Jesus would have replied in words something like these: 'I say thee nay, verily nay! It is as I have learned these words from childhood and have made them my own prayer, that I have shared that same experience of intimacy with God and known more fully each day the wonder and joy of God's presence in my life.' A major aspect of Jesus' teaching was that all humankind could know God in that same way. Two things which Jesus frequently stressed, as recorded in the Synoptic Gospels of Matthew, Mark and Luke, were that we could all trust in God unreservedly, and that we need never to be afraid. "Have faith in God!" and "Fear not!" are the most frequently recorded emphases in Jesus' ministry. I have tried to keep these two brief statements always in the back of my mind and I repeat them often as a kind of mantra, so that they guide my living. But again it is true, and it should always be kept well in mind, that Jesus was *not* the first person to make these emphases. The prophets of old from Moses and Joshua through to Isaiah and Micah as well as many of the Psalmists' words declare the same message: "In thee do I put my trust, O God" (*Psalm* 25: 2, *Psalm* 143: 8); and "In God I have put my trust; I will not fear what flesh can do unto me" (*Psalm* 56: 4). But to move even outside the Judeo-Christian tradition, I cite here a prayer from the Mahayana Buddhist tradition, a prayer that I feel quite sure Jesus would have willingly prayed had he known of its existence:

> O Thou who livest within our hearts,
> Awaken us to the immensity of thy Spirit,
> To the experience of thy living Presence!
> Deliver us from the bonds of selfish desires;
> From our slavery to small aims;
> From the delusion of narrow ego-hood.
> Enlighten us with the light of thy wisdom.
> Suffuse us with the incandescence of thy love;
> Give us strength to burst the sheath of our self-imposed
>   limitations;

So that we may awaken to a greater life:
The all-embracing life of thy love,
The all-embracing love of thy wisdom.

Let me sum up, then, the major emphases of this chapter thus far. I was brought up in a Christian home and was taught about Jesus from my earliest years of memory. I sang about Jesus as soon as I was able to sing. I am still an ardent follower of Jesus and will, I trust, speak "a good word" for him as long as I live. With such a background it is likely that Jesus will continue to be, as he has been, a major 'window' through which I will see something of the wonder of God's presence in human life. Jesus was *unique*. He was the only 'historical' teacher 'Jeshua' who lived and died in the earliest four decades of the Common Era, and about whose life and teachings we have some documentary evidence. Yet I am asserting that I do not believe that Jesus was unique in his practice of faith nor in his teaching about God and in his relationship with God. I do not believe that Jesus would have wanted to be thought of as being essentially different or superior to the great prophets of Israel. On one occasion when he was addressed as "Good Master", he replied, "Why call me 'good'? One only is good and that is God." (*Mark* 10: 17 & 18)

When at times I have expressed these views in public, I have usually been given a rejoinder such as, "So Jesus was *merely* a wonderful, insightful prophet, was he?" I do not believe that we should talk of a 'mere' prophet when referring to Jesus. That is like saying that J. S. Bach was a 'mere' composer of fugues. Both Jesus and Bach inspire a sense of awe, of wonder and of joy in those who attend to them in depth and commitment.

CHAPTER 1

I suggest that we will never attain to the fulfilment of the vision of a time when "The earth will be filled with the knowledge of God as the waters cover the sea" (*Isaiah* 11: 9), or when "No longer shall each person teach his neighbour, saying 'Know God (Yahweh),' for they shall *all* know me from the least to the greatest" (*Jeremiah* 31: 34), so long as we claim a kind of exclusive superiority for Christianity. For in orthodox Christianity it seems to be implicit that God desires all peoples to come into fellowship with Godself through Jesus the Christ. I once heard Krister Stendahl[5] say, in a panel discussion on Jewish-Christian relations, that he was not convinced that it was the good and perfect will of God that the earliest followers of Jesus and the synagogue should ever have separated. The ramifications of that thought deserve careful attention by the Church. As I have studied more carefully the testimonies of faith in God, not only by Jewish writers but also by Hindus, Muslims (especially the Sufi branch of Muslim spirituality), Sikhs, Buddhists, Taoists, and adherents of indigenous aboriginal spirituality (both Australian and North American), I have come to discover rich insights about the nature of God, of the Holy, in their thinking and living. I have been privileged to engage in deep conversations and to experience strong friendships with people of all the above religious commitments and am convinced of the genuine, lively experience of God's presence in their lives. As I believe it was the will of Jesus, God and God alone should be the centre of our faith; God, "whose centre is everywhere and whose circumference is nowhere", as I've heard some Quakers remark.

CHAPTER 2

Who Needs Jesus?

The title of this chapter was put into focus for me by two events which both occurred towards the end of December 1991. My dear friend, the Revd Dr. John Bodycomb (formerly Dean of the Uniting Church Theological Hall at Ormond College and Chaplain to the University of Melbourne) and his wife, Mavis, had attended the morning service at the Memorial Church, Harvard University, where the preacher was Rabbi Harold Kushner, author of the bestseller, *Why Bad Things Happen to Good People*. He also wrote a book called *Who needs God?* I have since wondered whether that was the title of his sermon that morning. John called me in Winnipeg to tell me what a worshipful, warm and stimulating experience it was. The sermon was full of 'good news', and he felt surges of deep joy flowing through the congregation. As he and Mavis were walking down the broad front steps of the church, Mavis nudged him and said, "Who needs Jesus?" A contemporary rabbi had just announced the good word of God's love and presence with power and authenticity in a Christian church.

A few days later, *The Christian Century* (Dec. 18–25) published a question-and-answer interview with Dr. John Dominic Crossan about his recent book, *The Historical Jesus: A Mediterranean Jewish Peasant* (Harper, 1991). When asked to expound on what he understood the essential message of Jesus to be, Dr. Crossan replied that at the heart of Jesus' message was a shared egalitarianism of material and spiritual resources. He stated that Jesus never said, "I bring you God's kingdom," but that the kingdom of God, 'unmediated' and 'unbrokered', was *present* for all to participate in. Neither he (Jesus) nor anyone else "had any monopoly or franchise on it", and that Jesus was telling his listeners in effect, "You don't even need me!"

Now, if in the considered opinion of one of the world's foremost New Testament scholars, and a committed Roman Catholic, *Jesus himself* was essentially saying "You don't need me even" in order fully to participate in God's family here and now, then the question "Who needs Jesus?" assumes a lively significance. Yet I need to draw the distinction between two different contexts in which the word 'need' is used. For I myself do indeed *need* Jesus to have lived and died. I have needed to know at least something about his work and teaching in order to be able to testify that I will always 'speak a good word' on his behalf. I have needed to have been powerfully influenced by his words and deeds to be able to state with deep sincerity that I follow him.

Yet more importantly still, our very civilisation, our educational, cultural, social, and human welfare institutions testify to the enormously important place the historical person of Jesus has had in the last two millennia. If we think about the arts, for example, this becomes clear. Numberless musical compositions, thousands of paintings in the world's major art galleries, many of the greatest works of poetry, and the writing of novels in the last few centuries, have all drawn inspiration from the life, the words, the ministry, and the death of that one man, Jesus. Granted that many of the above examples have also drawn their content from the dogmatic and theological interpretations of Jesus' life and death. For example, many of the texts of the great oratorios and cantatas include assertions of orthodox theological doctrines concerning Jesus. Mainline 'orthodox' Christianity has needed these views to be believed as true, in order to make the claims about Jesus that it does make.

That sense of the word 'need' as used in the above paragraphs, however, is of a very different nature, mood, and conviction from what mainline Christianity means when speaking about our need of Jesus. I am convinced, however, and with what I consider to be good reason and sound Biblical evidence, that many of the orthodox doctrines concerning Jesus' birth, deeds, his foreordained atoning death, his resurrection and 'second coming' are teachings of which Jesus himself, in his actual historical life, would not have approved. Although these claims have had power to convert, and although they are so deeply entrenched in the thinking and practice of Christian institutions and individuals as to seem impossible to challenge seriously, I nevertheless think that they should be challenged. Hence this book.

At the risk of being somewhat repetitive I am going to reiterate some of the major contents of what is sometimes referred to as 'the historic Christian faith' and then spell out some of my reasons for challenging it. Jesus is believed to have been sent to the earth by his 'Father', God, in order to die, to make a sacrifice of his life and thus *win* God's forgiveness for the sins of all humankind. He was believed to be 'the Eternal Son', the Second Person of the Holy Trinity, who with the Holy Spirit had existed, uncreated from eternity, beyond time. In taking upon himself the sins of the world, his death was a perfect, sufficient atonement and gained for all who would believe in him, salvation, which is why Jesus is referred to as 'the Saviour of the world'. Yet as a human being, "actual Jewish flesh" as Karl Barth put it in a lecture I heard him deliver (Princeton, 1962), his name was Jesus (in English, from the Greek *Iesous* and the Hebrew *Jehoshua*, sometimes shortened to *Jeshu* and anglicised as Joshua). As I pointed out in Chapter 1, this name means, and testifies to the fact that Yahweh (God) saves. In much Christian parlance salvation seems to refer mainly to salvation *from* sin, whereas in the Hebrew Scriptures it is seen more positively as the gift of God's grace and generosity whereby we are embraced in the fullness of God's *shalom*, the 'peaceable kingdom', and can experience that rich quality of life we may well call 'eternal' or full-orbed. I understand it as evident that in the teaching and preaching of Jesus, God and God alone is the central reality. God alone is our Saviour. In the story of Jesus' temptation, when the Devil asks Jesus to worship him, Jesus is recorded as replying, "Thou shalt worship Yahweh thy God, and *God only* shalt thou serve!"

Now, *if* the orthodox, traditional Christian faith as set out briefly above, is *in fact* the truth about Jesus, then we do indeed *need* Jesus in order to receive God's forgiveness and experience salvation. This belief is deeply dyed in the tradition. Two lines of an eighteenth-century hymn come to mind:

> Ashamed of Jesus? That dear friend
> On whom my hopes of heaven *depend*.[1]

A surface reading (and there are alternative interpretations) of a passage from John's Gospel (Ch. 14: 6), where Jesus is reported to have said, "No one comes to the Father except through me," seems to support the orthodox claim that we need Jesus if we are to receive God's forgiveness. That certainly seems to be the viewpoint of the author of that Gospel. The implication cannot be avoided that from *that* viewpoint it is God's will and intention that all the world's people should be Christians. *I do not think such a claim is in keeping with the mind of Jesus.* That all peoples would come to put their trust in God, in 'the Mystery of Love adored' (George Rawson), in the Holy One, yes, I believe Jesus would have desired that, but that all should be Christians I feel is an arrogance, though not intended as such by well-meaning Christians. Again, in a well known passage in The Letter to the Philippians, often thought to be an early Christian hymn, Paul seems to assert that it is God's will that all be Christians:

> ... God has given him [Jesus] a name that is above every other name, that at the name of Jesus *every* knee should bow, of things in heaven, and things on earth ... and every tongue confess that Jesus Christ is Lord, to the glory of God the Father.
>
> *Philippians* 2: 9-11.

I remind the reader that this book is only *my* testimony, it is not any kind of final truth (!!), yet I am urged to testify to a deep conviction that Jesus, who urged his hearers to put their trust unreservedly in God, would never have entertained the idea that all people should worship, bow the knee to, *him*. When Jesus spoke to the peasant villagers of southern Galilee, encouraging them to have a simple, childlike faith in God, as illustrated in stories and incidents recorded in the Gospels, I am convinced that he did not really believe deep down that their faith was in fact deficient because it did not take into account his role as the God-ordained sole mediator of that faith.

Furthermore the orthodox claim that God's forgiveness is essentially and irrevocably tied to Jesus' death as an atonement for sin seems not to take seriously the clear forthright proclamations of God's gracious, pardoning nature in the words of the Psalmists and prophets for centuries before the time of Jesus. These writers testify to a genuine experience of God's forgiving love.[2] When I put this to some of my orthodox friends, they have replied that God's forgiving love even prior to Jesus' death was nevertheless founded on God's eternal plan to have the incarnated 'eternal son' Jesus, in the fullness of time, die as the 'Lamb of God' (*John* 1: 29 & 36), who 'takes away the sin of the world'. They quote *Revelation* 13: 8, which speaks of "the Lamb slain from the foundation of the world." This interpretation of Jesus' death has, I believe, its basis in the application, by some of the earliest followers of Jesus, of Old Testament passages which they believed foretold the death of Jesus, in order to support the view that his death was intended by God to be for the world's salvation. This activity of interpreting Old Testament Scripture as applying to Jesus is called *midrash*[3] and the New Testament is full of it. One favourite passage used was *Isaiah* 53 which speaks of a Jewish figure known as 'the suffering servant of Yahweh', who was 'wounded for our transgressions', on whom 'Yahweh has laid the iniquity of us all', and who 'was brought as a *lamb* to the slaughter'. Anyone familiar with Handel's *Messiah* will recognise these words from *Isaiah* as the text for several choruses and one contralto solo. The suffering servant was never understood in Judaism as a Messianic kingly figure but rather as one in contradistinction to royalty. In the later Yiddish tradition he was a *lamed vovnik*, one of a company of "Just Men" who was willing to carry the sorrows and sins of his fellows and present them in his prayers to God who would accept and forgive.[4]

Let me make it clear; there is nothing wrong with *midrash* as a method of interpretation in and of itself. It was standard practice amongst rabbis at the time of Jesus who himself is recorded on a number of occasions as quoting Scripture to make his point, and it was a particular kind of *midrash* called a *pesher* in which the point was to show the later *fulfilment* of Scripture in current or expected events, which the community of Qumran made use of in the Dead Sea Scrolls' interpretations of the Jewish Scriptures. But in some ways it is too good a method to use to prove a point adamantly held. As the saying is, 'The devil himself can quote Scripture to his advantage.' I will try to show in a later chapter on Paul's role in interpreting the significance of Jesus' death, and in Appendix B, that it was largely due to Paul's fertile and in some ways brilliant mind that the atonement understanding of Jesus' death was first proclaimed. He had to answer the somewhat thorny question as to why, if Jesus was the Messiah, which Paul firmly believed, God allowed him to be executed. This was not part of Jewish Messianic expectation. I believe the case that Paul made convinced many other followers of Jesus because it gave a new impetus to their mission. I do not think the group in Jerusalem under Jesus' brother James was ever convinced of this interpretation but it spread like fire throughout the Greek world. Certainly the communities influenced by John took it up as we can see from the 'lamb of God' passages cited above, though Paul himself is not recorded as using that phrase. To my way of thinking, however, to claim that God's abundant forgiveness proclaimed in the Old Testament with such clarity as evidenced in words like, "As far as the east is from the west, so far has God removed our transgressions from us" (*Psalm* 103: 2, 3, & 12), was only available because in the eternal mind of God, Jesus' death was the historical enactment of 'the Lamb of God, slain from the foundation of the world' – such a claim seems to me to require a convoluted, 'fancy-footwork' method of shoring up a non-negotiable doctrine. It is like rescuing a drowning child for the sake of its clothes. Jesus, in teaching his disciples to pray "Forgive us our sins as we forgive those who sin against us," gave no hint that God's full and free forgiveness was dependent on him (Jesus) in some way.

It has also been suggested to me in a number of conversations that I reject the assertion that Jesus' death was, as one friend put it, a once-for-all eternal 'transaction' between God and humankind to enable the forgiveness of sin, because I do not regard sin seriously enough. That is simply not the case and I assure you that I'm not being defensive in saying that. I have never shrunk from using the word 'sin' in my teaching and preaching, but I take a wider, more radical view of the nature of sin than that which seems to me often to be understood. Sin is a far more serious matter than moral naughtiness and peccadilloes. There was a small placard on the wall of a Sunday School room I frequented as a little boy which stated "It is even a sin to steal a pin." I do not excuse trifling faults. Stealing is always wrong. Yet the constant emphasis on such 'sins' can breed what I believe is an unhealthy, essentially neurotic sense of guilt in our younger years with no growing sense of the deeper, more important aspects of sin. My parents and other elders who guided my youth were very concerned to warn me of the 'sins of the flesh'; sex before marriage, swearing, drunkenness and so forth, but I heard little about exploitation of the poor. We often made our breakfast coffee from 'Nescafe' tins which in those days were actually lined with tin. I was never reminded that the coffee beans had been picked by people who earned almost nothing for their labours, and the tin had been mined in jerry-built mines in South-East Asia where accidents were frequent and poor families had to do without their fathers who were killed in mine cave-ins. These situations were not spoken of in my youth and I was given no awareness of corporate sin.

The most important thing I learned about sin came from the lips of a teacher whose classes I attended at Harvard, Paul Tillich. He on several occasions said, "We have trivialised sin." He went on to remind us that two English words were derived from the Germanic word *sunde*: sin and asunder, and that sin is 'asunderness', alienation, broken relationships, in family life, in civic life, in national life, and globally. Alienations, broken relationships, can only be righted by reconciliation through justice, compassion and unconditional love. The Hebrew word for justice *tsedeq* means 'right relationships'. The life of Jesus provides us with a compelling pattern of compassionate acts, of care for society's outcasts, of championing the cause of the marginalised and destitute. Yes, I take sin seriously indeed, and I want to follow in his way of responding to it.

CHAPTER 2

One further matter that troubles me about the exclusive claims of the historic Christian faith with regard to Jesus' role as the one and only mediator between God and humankind (*1 Timothy* 2: 5) concerns the situation of other religious faiths. There are millions of faithful Jews, Hindus, Muslims, Buddhists and Taoists, to name some of the worldwide faiths and there are many more persons of faith who worship the Holy One and follow 'the Way' (the Tao, a concept very similar to 'the Word' in *John* 1: 1). Surely their sincere devotion is recognised by, and acceptable to, God, the Holy Spirit of Love and Justice. The apostle Peter even had this to say: "Truly I perceive that God shows no partiality, but that in every nation anyone who reverences God and does what is right is acceptable to God" (*Acts* 10: 34 & 35).

To sum up, then, my answer to the question, "Who needs Jesus?" is twofold. A yea and a nay. Jesus has had an incalculably great influence on our world's civilisations not only with regard to personal faith but in many other areas of culture, such as the arts, the pursuit of justice, freedom and peace. We *need* to acknowledge that. Yet we must also acknowledge that over the centuries, in some areas that same influence has been interpreted and misused to support bigotry, hatred, wars, and countless cases of inhumane injustice.

I believe, however, that John Dominic Crossan, cited above, was essentially correct when he stated that in announcing the presence of God's Kin(g)dom in our midst, Jesus claimed that in order to participate in that Kingdom, *"You don't even need me!"* Forgiveness, reconciliation between God and humankind, atonement for our erring ways, are the gifts of God's gracious nature alone. We do not require Jesus' death and resurrection to guarantee them.

CHAPTER 3

Was Jesus *the* Christ?

This chapter and the next one may be very disturbing to many Christian people. Yet I am seeking to be honest to the conclusions to which my conscience leads me after a careful study of the rise of the apocalyptic viewpoint as found in the intertestamental literature and also in a number of critical passages in the New Testament. According to many of the leading New Testament scholars, one of the major questions, if not *the* major question, raised in the earliest days of the community of Jesus' followers, was whether Jesus was the Christ or not. A surface reading of the books of the New Testament, with perhaps the exception of 'The General Epistle of James' and 'The Third Epistle of John', seems to indicate that by the time of the publication of these books the question has been answered resoundingly in the affirmative. Yet there have been highly respected scholars in my lifetime who call that affirmative answer into question, and I believe their convictions need careful attention. Over half a century ago the Revd Dr. W. R. Inge who formerly was Dean of St Paul's Cathedral, London, wrote:

> My own opinion is quite decided, but I doubt I should get the majority of scholars to agree with me. I believe that Jesus put himself in the succession of the prophets ... He lived, taught, and died as a prophet. The last thing that he wished to claim was to be Messiah, a disastrous political dream, the very thing he did not wish to encourage. But he made

such an overwhelming impression upon those who knew him that within a few years of his ignominious death his disciples loaded him with the highest honours they could think of ... they thought of him as the Messiah-designate, who was shortly to return in his own person, and send the Romans packing: 'Wilt thou at this time restore the kingdom to Israel?' (*Acts* 1: 6)[1]

Much more recently still, Professor Paula Fredriksen of the Boston University School of Theology is recorded as having said in an interview (2003):

> ... Nobody has a good explanation for why the term "Christ" attaches to the figure of Jesus. Scholars don't and the Gospels don't. I mean, all the Gospels are convinced that Jesus is the Christ, yet they all give different reasons why they thought so. The problem for scholars is this: Why did such a messianically improbable figure end up being known by *the* messianic title? He didn't do anything messianic. Messiahs don't cure people; messiahs aren't prophets. On the basis of what we have in the Gospels, Jesus is just not a messianic figure.[2]

There is, I believe, a good reason why Jesus came to be known as *the* Messiah. I will spell this out in a later chapter on Paul's understanding of Jesus.

It may be well at this point to look a little more closely at the term 'Christ' so as better to understand what kind of claim was being made for Jesus by those who asserted that he was the Christ. *Christos* is the Greek past-participle passive of the verb 'to anoint' and is a translation of the same participle in Hebrew, *moshiach*, the English form of which is 'messiah'. The word occurs in this participial (adjectival) form about 30 times in the Hebrew Scriptures,[3] but it is always joined directly to God, and in reference almost always to the kings of Israel and Judah who were anointed to their office. We have "the anointed of the God of Jacob"; "Yahweh's (the Lord's) anointed"; "*my* anointed" and "Thine anointed". All these instances are set within the normal historical passage of time, and carry a political, kingly reference. *Isaiah* 45: 1 even states that God had appointed the Persian ruler Cyrus as God's messiah! The use of the word 'messiah' in all these references is set in what I would call 'the prophetic' mode or mood. Israel's hopes were for another righteous king after the pattern of King David to ascend the throne and bring about the peaceful rule envisioned by the prophets as 'the Day of the Lord' or 'the Age to Come' in contrast to 'this present age'. 'This age' (*ha'olam ha zeh*) would be brought to a close and 'the age to come' (*ha 'olam ha ba'*) would arrive. At this time, "Swords would be beaten into ploughshares" (*Isaiah* 2: 4; and *Micah* 4: 3); "The wolf and the lamb would lie down together" (*Isaiah* 11: 6 and 65: 25); and "The earth would be filled with the knowledge of Yahweh (the Lord) as the waters cover the sea" (*Isaiah* 11: 9).

It is at this point that I want to introduce my approach to the question which is the title of this chapter: "Was Jesus *the* Christ?", an approach which I do not find made prominently elsewhere. In his remarkable, yet seldom referred to, book *Messianic Expectation in the Old Testament*,[4] German Dominican priest/scholar Joachim Becker asserts that there is *no* 'messianic expectation' in the Old Testament; no messianic expectation, that is, of the kind implied in the question reportedly put to Jesus: "Art thou *he that should come* or do we look for another?" (*Luke* 7: 19 & 20). Becker points out that the term '*the* Christ' standing alone as an epithet, as a title, occurs nowhere in the Old Testament. He states that it is only "on the threshold of the New Testament that we encounter *real* Messianism."[5] This real messianism, the expectation of a heaven-sent deliverer, not God's self, mark you well, but one acting as a vice-regent for God, and with both a redeeming and judging role, only developed with the rise of the apocalyptic viewpoint (in contrast to the 'prophetic' mood) in the 'intertestamental' period in the two centuries prior to the birth of Jesus. The prophets had called the people to responsible living in justice and mercy by which God's will would be done in and through the normal channels of history. The contrasting apocalyptic viewpoint or mood was strongly present during Jesus' lifetime and ministry, hence Ernst Kaesemann's famous dictum: "Apocalypticism was the matrix, the womb of Christian theology."[6] It was born out of the seeming *failure* of the prophetic mood's vision of "the age to come" being brought about through the agency of a faithful king, God's anointed one, and the righteous living of his subjects. The last king of Judah, Jehoiachin, was taken captive to Babylon with most of the inhabitants of Jerusalem when Nebuchadnezzar sacked the city, and he died there.

Yet even after the decades of the Exile, when Jerusalem was rebuilt, the hope of the dawn of God's "New Age" seemed desperately distant and dim. Eventually the alternative apocalyptic vision was born. God would break into this world's history and through the agency of a heaven-sent vice-regent who was titled *the* Messiah, the 'age to come' would be inaugurated and the hopes of the prophets' vision would be fulfilled. Let it be clear: if Jesus were believed to be *the*

Christ, he would be *the one who would bring about the end of 'this present age'*. This clearly did not happen. Dr. Albert Schweitzer, the scholar who insisted, at the turn of the twentieth century, that the studies on Jesus had not taken into account the dimension of the apocalyptic viewpoint and expectations, which were widely held and awaited at the time of Jesus, believed that *Jesus believed* himself to be that God-sent deliverer and that he expected God's intervention to establish 'the Age to Come' to occur in his lifetime. Schweitzer thought that when Jesus sent his disciples out to preach and heal in the hamlets of southern Galilee, he believed *that* activity would initiate the end of the present age: "You will not have gone through all the towns of Israel before the Son of Man comes" (*Matthew* 10: 23b). Yet Jesus' prediction and expectation was *not* fulfilled. Jesus therefore took it upon *himself*, said Schweitzer, so to act provocatively that he would compel the Pharisees and the rulers to get rid of him and by going to the Cross to suffer, he expected that God would honour his messianic role and bring in, in a supernatural way, the Kingdom, the Parousia, the 'coming of the Son of Man' who was to be manifested as Jesus himself.[7] This supernatural intervention simply did *not* occur and Jesus died, said Schweitzer, a deluded, mistaken apocalyptic figure, with the words, "My God, my God, why hast thou forsaken me?" on his lips. To cite Schweitzer a little more fully:

> Jesus comes, and in the knowledge that he is the coming Son of Man lays hold of the wheel of the world to start it moving on that last revolution which is to bring all ordinary history to a close. It refuses to turn, and he throws himself upon it. Then it does turn; and crushes him ... The wheel

rolls onward, and the mangled body of *the one immeasurably great Man*, who was strong enough to think of himself as the spiritual ruler of mankind and to bend history to his purpose, is hanging upon it still.[8]

"That", says Schweitzer, "is his victory. For a mighty spiritual force streams forth from him and flows through our time also."[9] Still "as of old, by the lake-side, he came to those who knew him not. He speaks to us the same words: 'Follow me!'"[10] I and millions of others have experienced that 'mighty spiritual force' and have been through the ages and still are to this day committed followers of Jesus. If Schweitzer's understanding of Jesus' life, ministry and death is correct, then it is also clear that Jesus historically was *not* the Christ. But for Schweitzer, who Jesus was historically is not of great importance. The importance of Jesus lies in 'the spiritual force that streams forth from him.'

I emphasise again that the term, the title, *the* Christ was born of apocalyptic thinking; it was coined by adherents of that movement and takes its meaning from within that framework. It stands for a very specific person with a very specific role to play and function to fulfil, namely, as Schweitzer, cited above, put it: 'to bring all ordinary history to a close', and inaugurate the 'age to come' when wars shall be no more and peace shall flood the earth. That is what the title '*The Christ*' was intended, by those who coined it and first used it, to mean. I don't believe we should try to bend it to mean something different, nor spiritualise it and try to show how it still applies to Jesus. Clearly, in terms of the title's true point of reference, Jesus was not *the* Christ. I believe that no apocalyptically-orientated Jew in Jesus' day – and that would apply to Pharisaic synagogue adherents –

would have seen Jesus at the time of his execution as the Messiah. For the events which the Messiah would have set in motion simply *had not happened.*

After all the centuries during which Christianity has flourished, however, it seems almost impossible to separate the word 'Christ' from the person of Jesus. Most believers would argue that since these two words are almost always found together in the New Testament, the witness of those documents indicates that the matter is settled. Yet there are anomalies with regard to the use of the title 'Christ' as applying to Jesus *in the New Testament itself.* Two of the twentieth century's major New Testament scholars, the late Bishop J. A. T. ('Honest-to God') Robinson of Cambridge University and Lutheran Bishop Krister Stendahl of Harvard University, both argued that the earliest testimony concerning Jesus was that even after his death and so-called resurrection, Jesus was *not yet* the Christ but was still only the Messiah-designate, the Christ-elect. They both argue from the text of a speech Peter is recorded as making in *Acts* 3: 12-21, especially vv. 19-21. Peter is calling on the gathered crowd in Jerusalem to repent for having denied and killed the 'Just One' (Jesus, vv. 14 & 15), acting albeit in ignorance (v. 17); to repent "so that God shall send the Christ proclaimed beforehand to you, namely Jesus whom the heavens must retain until the restitution, the renewal of all things [the Age to Come] which God has spoken by the mouths of the prophets" (vv. 20 & 21). Peter then continues referring to Jesus as *the prophet* like unto Moses whom Moses predicted would come (vv. 23 & 24). Robinson, in a landmark essay 'The Most Primitive Christology of All?'[11] commenting on this *Acts* passage, writes:

Jesus is here still only the Christ-*elect*; the Messianic age has yet to be inaugurated. If we put the question, "Art thou 'he that should come', or do we look for another?", the answer which this speech (of Peter) seems to be giving is, "Yes, Jesus *is* 'the one who shall come'. We know who the Messiah *will be*; there is no need to look for another. To be sure, the Messiah is *still to come*."[12]

If Robinson's tightly argued case as concluded in the quotation above is correct, and I believe it is, what are we to make of it? Peter assures those in his audience that if they truly repent God will send Jesus, who is to be the Christ appointed for them and 'the Age to Come' will dawn. We do not know how the people responded to Peter's urgent call to repentance. We *do know* that God did *not* send Jesus as the Christ at that time, nor ever since! From this situation the doctrine of 'The Second Coming' was developed. The term 'The Second Coming' does not appear in the New Testament; the term used for that speculated event is the *parousia* which is translated as 'presence' (its actual meaning) or as 'coming' (its interpreted meaning). In his book, *The Apostolic Preaching*, the late Professor C. H. Dodd suggested that the core of the message is to be found in Peter's speech in *Acts* 2: 22-24:

> Jesus of Nazareth, *a man approved by God* among you by miracles and wonders and signs, which God did by him in your midst ... Him being delivered by the predeterminate counsel and foreknowledge of God, ye have taken, and by wicked hands have crucified and slain: Whom God hath raised up, having loosed the pains of death ...

The Second Coming is not a part of that core proclamation. It became a *necessary* part of later preaching in order to answer the anomaly described above.[13]

In lectures at Harvard which I attended, Professor Stendahl spoke of this same *Acts* 3 passage as proclaiming what he called 'the *will-be*-ness' of Jesus as the coming Christ. He went on to say that as the early communities of Jesus' followers grew and spread, this 'will-be-ness' was read back into the 'is-ness' of Jesus as Christ, as proclaimed in *Acts* 2: 32-36 by Peter: "God has made him Lord and Christ, this Jesus whom you crucified and whom God raised up." This from the same Peter who is recorded in the next chapter as declaring that Jesus was *not yet* the Christ. Yet even before Jesus' death, this same Peter again had already confessed that Jesus was the Christ, and in Matthew's record, Jesus had fully approved of Peter's words, "Thou *art* the Christ", replying, "Blessed are you, Simon son of Jonas" (*Matthew* 16: 16 & 17). If, however, we look at the same incident as recorded in the earlier written Gospel of Mark, a rather different mood seems evident (*Mark* 8: 27-33). Here Peter is *not* roundly approved of by Jesus, but is rebuked with the words, "Thou savourest not the things that be of God." In *Matthew*, Jesus commanded the disciples 'to tell no one that he was *Jesus the Christ*'; it was to be kept secret. But in *Mark* just before he rebuked Peter he commanded the disciples that they should 'tell no one of him'. But tell no one *what* about him? *That he was the Christ, apparently*, because hundreds of folk knew who Jesus, the preacher and healer, was. The five words in the Greek text translated as 'that they tell no one concerning him' may as well be construed as "Don't you go saying *that* (i.e. that he was the Christ) about me to anyone!" Such was the likely reply by Jesus to Peter and the disciples as suggested to me by the Australian Marcan scholar, the late Dr. Robert Maddox of Sydney.[14]

CHAPTER 3

The point I am emphasizing in spelling out these various anomalous New Testament statements concerning Jesus' claim to the title '*the* Christ' is that it is evident that the New Testament does not unequivocally assert the Messiahship of Jesus. Even though these documents were published several decades after Jesus' death, by which time the terms 'Jesus' and 'Christ' are almost always found together, we have noticed that there are passages which call the assumption that Jesus was the Christ into question, passages which may well reflect the thinking of earlier years following Jesus' life and death when his role as *the* Christ was by no means taken for granted by all his followers. Need it really affect the liveliness of our faith in God or our commitment to follow Jesus' way if Jesus did not fulfil the role of '*the* Christ'? Peter urgently called on the people to repent in order that *the* Christ could be sent to them. But why be so urgent about it, and of how much importance was that 'coming' to Peter's hearers, if two thousand years later '*the* Christ' has still not been sent? If Dean Inge, cited above, was correct in his opinion, Jesus didn't want to be *the* Christ, anyway.

Chapter 4

Jesus and *the* Resurrection

In the previous chapter I wrote about the rise of the apocalyptic viewpoint. The visions of the prophets of a time when "the earth would be filled with the knowledge of God", and "wars would be no more", seemed never to be coming to fulfilment through the normal channels of Israel's history. Thus it came to be believed that God would intervene in human history by sending *the* Christ to put an end to this present age and inaugurate "the Day of the Lord", the "Kingdom of God" on earth. This we call the apocalyptic viewpoint. People came to be expecting "he that should come" to put an end to the distresses caused by Israel's opponents, and in particular, to the Roman occupation of their land.

The major impulse behind the apocalyptic vision was a deep longing to see the *justice* of God as proclaimed by the prophets actually coming to pass. The theological term for this is *theodicy*,[1] the justice, the fairness of God. It is not often enough emphasized that theodicy is the antecedent of apocalypticism, but the recognition of this is essential to our understanding of the significance of *the* resurrection. For the terms '*the* Christ' and 'the resurrection' are bound inextricably together in the apocalyptic vision. For how would it be just and fair if, when God sent the Christ to inaugurate the New Age, all those in the past who had longed for and worked for that great day were not permitted to be present and share in it? Thus was born the belief in *the* Resurrection which was understood to be a corporate event; "the dead" in the Greek phrase "the resurrection of the dead" is always plural (*tōn nekrōn*). Nowadays we put the qualifying adjective in the phrase when it is referred to, and call it "the general resurrection". But there was no qualifying adjective needed for the term as it was initially used. It was coined to stand for a very specific event which was to occur when *the* Christ would come. It was apocalyptic Judaism's term and I do not believe we have the right to bend it to make it mean something else.

Just as the evidence which I put before you in the previous chapter would seem to indicate, namely, that Jesus did not fulfil the role of *the* Christ, though Peter stated he would shortly do so if the people were to obey his urgent plea for repentance,[2] so likewise, and contingently so, I hope it can be seen, *the* resurrection, that is, of course, the general resurrection, *did not happen!* Matthew's Gospel, written some forty or more years later, states that it or something like it did happen following Jesus' resurrection: "And the graves were opened, and many bodies of the saints which slept arose, and came out of the graves and went into the holy city and appeared unto many" (*Matthew* 27: 52 & 53). No other New Testament writer supports this story. One would think that if it did occur, and publicly, apparently, it would have been so memorable that it would have been spoken of very widely; but no, no other reference to it appears.

If the story of Peter's speech in *Acts* 3, of which I have written in the previous chapter, is historical, and Jesus had *not yet* been sent by God as *the* Christ, then since the resurrection (that is, the general resurrection) was only to occur at the coming of *the* Christ, it follows that *that* event had *not yet* occurred. But what then of Jesus' so-called resurrection? Was it a 'one-off' event, a foretaste? There was no Jewish tradition of *the* Christ having to suffer and die before God would raise all the faithful dead so that they might participate in 'the Age to Come'.[3] St. Paul was at least still faithful to the Jewish apocalyptic tradition when he stated categorically that Jesus' resurrection and the general resurrection were inextricably bound together: "But if there be no resurrection of the dead, then is Christ not risen" (*1 Corinthians* 15: 13). "They stand or fall together," in the words of John Dominic Crossan, who goes on to say, "It never occurs to Paul that Jesus' resurrection might be a special or unique privilege given to him because he is Messiah... Risen apparitions are, for Paul, not about the *vision* of a dead man but about the vision of a dead man who *begins the general resurrection of the dead*"[4] (italics mine). In the same vein Crossan writes, "We often say that for Paul the end of the world was imminent. It is more accurate to say that for Paul the end had already begun; only its final consummation was imminent."[5] But Paul was wrong about that, was he not? We would have to stretch the meaning of 'imminent' beyond all reason to make it refer to something which might happen 2000 or more years ahead. Similarly with Peter's urgent plea for the people to repent "so that God would send the Christ, namely Jesus ..." Why be *urgent* about the need to repent, when that predicted event has not even yet happened? I do not believe that it ever will happen, nor that it was God's intention for humankind's history. I assert that both Paul and Peter misspoke – not lied or spoke dishonestly, but that their sincere beliefs about the end of this world's history were simply wrong. The context in which both Peter and Paul are recorded as speaking about the end of the age makes it clear to me that they both expected this glorious event to be soon, hence the urgency of Peter's appeal. Paul, in what I believe to be the earliest written documents we have of that time, namely, the Thessalonian correspondence (49 or 50 in the Common Era), seems to believe that he himself will be present when that great day arrives: "The dead in Christ shall rise first, and then *we* who are alive and remain will be caught up together with them to meet the Lord in the air" (*1 Thess*. 4: 16 & 17). This was a glorious vision but it did not happen, and I believe it never will.

Yet believers who still recite the Creed which states, "And he shall come again in glory to judge both the living and the dead," may well respond to the centuries of delay as did the writer of *2 Peter* in response to those who sceptically scoffed, "Where is the promise of his coming?" They, moreover, were only about one century removed from the days of Jesus' life. The epistle writer answered, "Do not be ignorant of this fact: a thousand years with God is as one day." I do not find that kind of explanation very satisfactory. Yet as to Jesus' resurrection being the beginning of the general resurrection, most Christians believe that *something happened* on what we now call Easter morning. When we have been brought up in communities of the Christian faith, this is a difficult belief to call into question. It is proclaimed constantly in worship. All the Gospels agree that the dead body of Jesus was 'resurrected'. None of them, however, claim that anyone saw Jesus coming out of the tomb when God 'raised' him. Furthermore *only believers* testified to have seen him or been with him after he was said to be alive again. John's Gospel records a scene where the one 'doubter', Thomas, is invited to put his hands into Jesus' wounds incurred by his crucifixion. This incident has the hallmarks of a Johannine symbolic action similar to Jesus' turning water into wine. A strong theological statement is made: the disciple must identify with Jesus' death; but I reject its historicity. John's Gospel was from early times called the 'spiritual' Gospel. The Synoptic Gospels make no mention of 'doubting Thomas' and this is an amazing incident, one which I would have thought so memorable that all the Gospel writers would mention it.

Some of my closest friends have responded to what they regard as my 'scepticism' with respect to the historicity of Jesus' resurrection, by asking, "How did it happen that a band of frightened disciples developed over night, as it were, into a fearless group of witnesses to the Messiahship of Jesus?" That is a fair question but my answer to it is itself a question. Where do we get the evidence that there was a group of *frightened* disciples? My reading of some of the research of Professor Paula Fredriksen of Boston University suggests otherwise.[6] In a seminar which I chaired in the 1990s, John Dominic Crossan, our guest, stated his opinion that at the time of the crucifixion, many of the disciples were in southern Galilee announcing the presence of the Kingdom as they travelled from hamlet to hamlet. In the vigorous discussion which followed Dr. Crossan's presentation, one of the student members present asked what those disciples would have said or done if they had been told that Jesus had very recently been executed in Jerusalem. Dr. Crossan said that he believed they would have said something like "We are tremendously saddened to hear that, but we must get on with the work Jesus instructed us to do." If Crossan is right then those disciples do not sound like a frightened group of men and women.

That brings me to the central issue I wish to raise. The only documentary evidence we have with respect to the Messiahship of Jesus and his resurrection is the New Testament: the statements in the *Gospels*, the *Acts of the Apostles*, and the *Epistles*, chiefly those of St. Paul. A document's own testimony as to its historical accuracy and truth must raise questions, surely, if corroborative evidence independent of the New Testament writers' convictions is not forthcoming. There *is* evidence for Jesus' life and death in the writings of Josephus and others, but only of *rumours* amongst Jesus' followers about his still, or again, being alive: rumours not accepted as historical by non-New Testament writers. But again my critics answer, "Surely you are not suggesting that the New Testament writers are guilty of deliberately propagating an untruth, a hoax, are you? Why, if you reject the fact of Jesus' resurrection, are you not denying the central fact of our faith? Are you not 'throwing out the baby with the bath-water'?" There are two issues here.

No, I am not suggesting that a deliberate lie or hoax was being proclaimed by the New Testament writers. I do believe, however, some of the earliest followers of Jesus in their enthusiastic recollections of the influence of his wonderful life and teachings on their own lives, grew to have mistaken convictions about who their executed leader really was.[7] In Chapter 6, I will suggest how that Paul played a pivotal role in the development of the doctrines of Jesus' Messiahship and his resurrection. I return, however, to the undeniable fact that it is only in the New Testament documents that we find the earliest assertions of these doctrines. Moreover, we need to remember that none of these documents were written or circulated prior to almost two decades after Jesus' death and that the Gospels were probably published at least two decades later still.

Some have asked me, "How could the record be untrue, since it has flourished for nearly two thousand years?" I do not find that so great a problem. I have had in my classes several Mormons. They were great people and good students whose convictions were as strong as those of orthodox Christians. They believe Jesus had a later mission in North America and look upon *The Book of Mormon* as *The Second Testament of Jesus Christ*. I do not believe that to be true and nor will many of my readers, I'm sure. Yet their church is flourishing all around the world. I also have a good number of Muslim friends and colleagues who believe the Koran is the Word of God without error. I respect their view but cannot believe it. Yet Islam is the fastest growing faith in the world. The flourishing of the doctrines of Jesus' Messiahship and his Resurrection does not guarantee their truth. I reiterate that my critique of those two doctrines is based on the understanding of those terms as they were originally developed and coined in the pre-Christian growth of apocalyptic Judaism, and I find no reason for changing the historical meaning of those terms.

Now to the allegation that I am 'throwing out the baby with the bath-water'. In that phrase the 'baby' is the reality who must be saved or retained. The 'bath-water' is peripheral and can be dispensed with. Now for me, the realities to be retained are the presence of our faithful *God*, and the inspiration of the life and death of Jesus who unflinchingly trusted in God. No one who reads this book could possibly say that I am throwing out the testimony to the faithfulness of God, nor to the person of Jesus as a wonderful guide to the life of faith in God. Acceptance of the doctrines of Jesus' Messiahship and his Resurrection can, and I believe, should, be dispensed with in the task of enlarging our understanding of the Kin(g)dom of God where devout, just, and merciful Jews, Hindus, Muslims, Buddhists and many others all have an equal place.

As I have stated above, the New Testament documents which assert that Jesus was the Christ and that God raised him from the dead do contain testimonies that do seem to call into question their historical truth. We found a distinct variation between at least two of Peter's recorded assertions regarding Jesus' Messiahship. In the *Matthew* 16 passage Jesus is stated to be already 'the Christ'; in the *Acts* 3 passage he is only as yet 'the Messiah-designate' whom God *will send* as Christ if the people repent. The two testimonies cannot both be true. In a similar fashion there seem to be conflicting testimonies as to the resurrection-body of Jesus. Luke has Jesus insisting after his resurrection that he was not a 'spirit' or 'ghost' as the 'frightened' disciples had supposed: "... a spirit has not flesh and blood as you see me have" (*Luke* 24: 39). Later, Paul, when asked "How are the dead raised up, and with what body do they come?" (*1 Cor.* 15: 35), concludes that the resurrected body is *not* "flesh and blood" (*1 Cor.* 15: 50). Paul of course had not read the supposed words of Jesus in *Luke* 24: 39, cited above, for that document would not have been published until about two decades after Paul's words were written. Did the Gospel writers believe in the physical resurrection of Jesus? Apparently, yes. Did Paul? Apparently, no. Many believers, including noted scholars, think of the event as 'spiritual' – a *vision* given to, or experienced by, believers – *not*, however, an hallucination. Many others cling to the Gospel post-resurrection stories as literal history. The superb, though as I believe, mistaken Christian apologist, C. S. Lewis, wrote in one place that the resurrected Jesus had a body, 'the resurrection-body', which functioned differently from his pre-crucifixion body. It could pass through walls and suddenly appear to the disciples in the upper room where they were gathered (*John* 20: 19). I respect this as the view of an ardent, committed believer in the Resurrection. This brings me to my conclusions with respect to the historicity of Jesus' Resurrection.

If God did not raise Jesus from the dead, then how did the New Testament assertion of the Resurrection come about? I emphasize again that I do not believe the writers were knowingly proclaiming untruths, deliberately perpetrating a hoax. I believe the assertions of two previously cited scholars give us a reliable clue as to why and how the stories, the convictions, amongst some of the followers of Jesus developed. Albert Schweitzer, readers will recall, after speaking of Jesus' ignominious death, added that "a mighty spiritual force streamed forth from him and still flows through our time." He makes *no mention* in this context of a resurrection, mark you well. In fact he states, "It is not Jesus in his historic actuality ... one who is significant for us ... but the *spirit* which issues from him."[8] I believe the impulse which fostered the experience of Jesus' continuing presence, the 'resurrection-experience', was the working in the minds and lives of some of the close followers of Jesus of that 'mighty spiritual force' of which Schweitzer writes. Likewise,

Dean W. R. Inge, after asserting his conviction that the last thing Jesus would have wanted was to be hailed as 'the Christ', added that "the *overwhelming* impression Jesus had made on his followers was such that within a few years of his death his disciples loaded him with the *highest honours* they could think of." [9] They were led to proclaim him as the Messiah, the inaugurator of God's New Age, as the first-fruits of 'the resurrection of the dead' (*1 Corinthians* 15: 20 & 23).

As more and more of the early followers of Jesus came to be convinced, to a considerable extent, I believe, through the influence of Paul's thinking, of both the Messiahship of Jesus and his resurrection from the dead, a great activity of searching ('midrashing') the Old Testament Scriptures took place. This work set out to show that both Jesus' Messiahship and his Resurrection had been predicted by the compilers of the Torah, by the Psalmists and by the Prophets. Many of these applications of the Hebrew Scriptures to demonstrate their fulfilment in the life of Jesus are considered by most scholars to have been taken out of context and in some cases quite erroneously interpreted. A case in point would be *Matthew* 2: 15's citation of *Hosea* 11: 1: "Out of Egypt I have called my son;" a specious example of *midrash*, bending Hosea's context quite mistakenly. This activity continues still in much preaching and liturgy, especially in hymn and oratorio texts. A prime example can be seen, I believe, in the Old Testament texts used in Handel's *Messiah*, where in an aria "I Know that My Redeemer Liveth" the listener is led to believe that Jesus' resurrection was predicted by Job: "Though worms destroy this body, yet in my flesh I shall see God" (*Job* 19: 25 & 26). The Hebrew text of *Job* cannot possibly mean what this English translation makes it appear to mean. Anyway, Job has just declared categorically in a previous chapter that there is no life after death for humankind (*Job* 14: 10-12). I have made this case in some detail in Appendix 'A' in this book, if the reader wants further confirmation of this conclusion. But to return to my initial point: this Old Testament interpretive activity seemed to confirm for many early followers of Jesus, and account in no small way to the development of, most of the Christian faith's credal beliefs which became so enshrined as to be impregnable against argument, non-negotiable in debate. In my view the influence of Paul, as stated above, in this development is of pivotal importance.

Schweitzer, in the passage just cited (note 8) seems to downplay the kind of detail about what actually happened in Jesus' life which I have been discussing in this chapter. More recently the contemporary scholar Marcus Borg apparently agrees with Schweitzer's view that "it is not Jesus as historically known ... who is significant for our time." Borg writes, "Knowledge of the historical Jesus is *not essential*."[10] He states that we are not required to have "accurate historical information" or "correct beliefs about the historical Jesus." I strongly dissent from this 'ahistorical' viewpoint. Schweitzer and Borg notwithstanding, I believe that the facts about the historical Jesus, as accurately as we have evidence to discern their probability, are of *essential importance* if we are concerned for the *truth*. I believe that the words and deeds of the historical Jesus are what should inspire us to follow him.

CHAPTER 5

More, more about Jesus

I have written in Chapters 1 and 2 about what I believe were the central teachings of Jesus, namely, that we can trust in God without reserve and thus be free of all fear. I want now to write more about Jesus' deeds, his relationships with others, his deep compassion towards the poor, the oppressed, the outcasts and dispossessed in the society in which he lived, and above all, his uncompromising concern for *justice* as a major aspect of God's kingdom. Jesus was, as one hymnwriter has expressed it, 'a young and fearless prophet.' We do not have many clear instances given in the Gospels, as they currently stand, of Jesus' commitment to social justice. We find more explicit attitudes in this regard in the words of the Old Testament prophets. Yet I believe that Jesus followed the demands that these earlier writers made in God's name very closely. We perhaps should look more carefully at Jesus' parables to find probable clues to the evidence of Jesus' radical insistence on social justice.

Here I rely heavily on the parable research of the American scholar, Professor William Herzog, as set out in his book, *Parables As Subversive Speech: Jesus as Pedagogue of the Oppressed*.[1] Herzog accepts the stories themselves as they actually appear in the Gospels, but suggests that the normally understood interpretations of them by the New Testament writers/editors, and by preachers down through the ages, have seemed to 'soft-pedal' the radical indictments against injustice which many of the parables in their original setting carried. Herzog begins his opening chapter with these salient words:

> This study of the parables poses a problem that can be expressed in a series of questions: What if the parables of Jesus were neither theological nor moral stories but political and economic ones? What if the concern of the parables was not the reign of God but the reigning systems of oppression that dominated Palestine in the time of Jesus? What if the scenes they presented were not stories about how God works in the world but codifications about how exploitation worked in Palestine ... exposing exploitation rather than revealing justification? What would all this mean for a reading of the parables?[2]

Let me give an illustration of this viewpoint based on the well-known parable of the talents (*Matthew* 25: 14-30). The master or nobleman, on leaving his property in order to journey to a 'far country', gave three of his agents or stewards sums of money and commanded them to use it to make as much profit as they could for their master in his absence. One steward, who apparently had been a successful money-lender in the past, was given five talents, another received two, and the third steward just one talent. When I was a parish pastor, both in South Australia and in New Hampshire, U.S.A., I used this parable as the basis for my sermon on what was then called 'Stewardship Sunday'. I would say something like this: "Not many of us are in the five or two talent bracket. Mostly we are in the one talent category. We have limited financial resources and cannot lay claim to fame in other aspects of our lives. We must *not*, however, allow those facts to 'let us off the hook' with regard to our use of what we *do* have in the way of talents and substance. The 'master', God or Jesus, will require of us an account of our stewardship of the abilities and money we do have, just as the one-talent man in the parable was required to give account for his use of the talent given him. Now there is nothing wrong in making such a point in a sermon. It is true that we should use what we have wisely and generously. Yet Herzog insists that this was *not* the point of the parable in its original context, which was the agricultural economy and its practices in southern Galilee. If we had read the story more carefully we should have realized that. In my early sermon interpretation, the master or landlord was God or perhaps Jesus. In the parable, however, when the one-talent servant returns the full amount given him to his master, he says, "I knew you were a hard man who reaped where you had not sown, and profited where you had not laboured nor invested!" Does that sound like a description of God or Jesus? I say thee *nay*! The landlord was a typical large property owner belonging to the Roman occupation population. The land had originally been small lots owned by Jewish farmers. When bad seasons had repeatedly occurred the rich Roman had bought out at a cheap price the small land-owning farmers, but had allowed the farmers to remain as tenants, requiring of them, however, a large percentage of any profit they made from their produce. When poor seasons recurred, the landlord would, through his stewards, offer further loans at exorbitant interest to the poor tenants so that they could afford to buy more seed and keep on farming. Eventually the tenant farmers, after more poor seasons, could never pay back the loans and were reduced to becoming beggars. I'm not making this up. There is ample documentary evidence from those times to support the view that this was how the system worked. It is the old story of the rich growing richer and the poor, poorer.

Jesus lived in this part of the world and was enraged by the gross injustice done to many of fellow country folk. As Jesus told the story, he was supporting the dispossessed and *calling for dissent* against such injustice at the risk of being roundly condemned by the Roman authorities for so acting. In Jesus' view, states Herzog, and I believe he is right, the one-talent man is the courageous *hero* of the story. He was not going to play into the hands of the rich, heartless, greedy overlord. He would not lend the money given to him to his poor fellow Jewish tenant farmers only to see them reduced to beggary. He was 'the whistle blower'[3] calling attention to the wrongness, the injustice of the whole system, and he paid a high price for his courage – as indeed did Jesus in his support for the oppressed, in the cause of social justice. The Roman governing authorities did not want any dissenting uprising on the part of the Jewish common-folk. The message from this story/act of Jesus is that we are called, as his followers, to be 'whistle-blowers', exposing injustice fearlessly wherever we see it.

Recently, I heard a sermon on the story of the widow who cast two mites into the treasury. Jesus is reported by Mark and Luke as saying that her gift was greater than all the gifts of the rich. The preacher, The Revd Dr. Philip Carr, in the same vein as Herzog, suggested that the words put on Jesus' lips by Mark, while expressing deep approval of the widow's unconditional generosity, were not, in his view, the likely reaction to the situation by the historical Jesus. He believed that it would have been much more likely that Jesus was outraged by the fact that the widow was so poorly provided for by the society she lived in that she only had two mites to give. I am inclined to believe that Dr. Carr's interpretation comes nearer to the mind of Jesus who fearlessly followed the way of the prophets who relentlessly inveighed against those who robbed widows of their rights.[4]

A plain surface reading of other parables gives us ample evidence of various aspects of Jesus' concern. Compassion towards those in need of help is illustrated in the so-called 'Good Samaritan' story (*Luke* 10: 30-37). Unconditional love and forgiveness are at the heart of the story of 'The Prodigal Son' (*Luke* 15: 11-24). The need for alertness and a warning not to treat God's grace carelessly or cheaply can be seen in the story of 'The Wise and Foolish Bridesmaids' (*Matthew* 25: 1-13). That for Jesus *deeds* are more important than words is emphasized in the story of the father who asked his two sons to help him work in the field (*Matthew* 21: 28-31). In short, the teaching of Jesus as found in his parables presents us with a comprehensive picture of his attitudes and activities; a compendium of the kinds of deeds required of us as his followers.

We need to consider further Jesus' relationship with God as it bears upon his own self-understanding. Credal, orthodox Christianity asserts that Jesus was God incarnate while at the same time, while in the flesh, "emptying himself" (see *Philippians* 2: 7 & 8) of such generally accepted aspects, abilities and qualities of God, such as omniscience, omnipotence and omnipresence. What then does it mean to be 'God-in-the-flesh' without such capacities which most believers normally assert to belong to God? Many Christians are of two minds in this area of belief. Could Jesus have suspended the normal experience of our bodies sinking in water because he was God, thus enabling him to walk on the surface of the water in Lake Galilee? I have known quite a few highly academically trained persons who sincerely believe that Jesus actually walked on the water and turned jars of water at Cana's wedding feast into jars of wine. I cannot identify with the humanity of a Jesus who can and does perform such acts. I also know of many highly intelligent Christians, essentially orthodox in belief, who nevertheless regard such acts symbolically, not literally. Orthodoxy asserts Jesus' *full* humanity and at the same time, in the same person, *full* Deity. I find this to be as impossible a notion, logically, as that of a square circle. Did Jesus believe himself to be God's very self? I cannot believe it of him. The writer of The Epistle to the Hebrews speaks of Jesus as "tempted *in all points* like as we are, *yet without sin*" (*Hebrews* 4: 15).

I cannot speak for others, but for me, the hardest temptations to resist are in areas where I have *already fallen* for the temptation. *If* Jesus *never* fell for any temptation then he, by definition, was *not* tempted 'in all points' like I have been. The doctrine of 'the sinlessness of Jesus' which needs to be true if he were 'very God of very God' seems to me to detract from his full humanity; it puts him in a category, as far as his humanity is concerned, different from every other human being who has ever lived. He would not have been really one of us. That seems to suit orthodoxy but it is not an article of my faith.

Earlier I cited Marcus Borg's view expressed in his article, "What Did Jesus Know?", that whatever else he did or did not know, Jesus certainly knew God.[5] As I understand him, he lived his life in an intimate relationship with God, whom he called 'my father'. He communed with God who was for him a deeply personal, knowable reality. He 'practised the presence of God' in his daily life and he taught his followers that they could live in the same kind of relationship with God. I believe this to be true and it is one of the major areas in which I earnestly try to follow Jesus. A leading Quaker, Dr. Paul Lacey speaks of 'attending to the promptings of the Inward Teacher'. I have found this to be a most helpful way of practising God's presence daily, following the way of Jesus. *Knowing* God is for me the most important 'knowledge' of any human person's experience, but it does not, in my view, necessarily require the explicit use of the word 'God', which for many has been rendered suspect by the complicated arguments of systematic theology and by people claiming 'God' on their side to 'prove' the rightness of their actions.

Yet we must be honest and say that Jesus knew God intimately but in the *context* of his historical existence as a Galilean Jewish peasant of a charismatic turn of mind in the early decades of the Common Era. He most probably believed that Moses wrote the first five books of what we call the Old Testament, and that King David wrote many, if not most, of the Psalms. Both propositions are highly unlikely to be true. I believe he had absolutely no idea that a human being could ever travel physically to the moon, nor that there was on earth an island-continent, now called Australia, whose inhabitants, at that time, had no knowledge of the spiritual contributions of the Hebrew people, though I believe they had very real experiences of the presence of 'the Holy' in their lives. Jesus almost certainly believed that God, his 'Father' had created the world, the physical universe in which he lived, a fact which for me does not mean that as a follower of Jesus I should hold the same belief about the universe's existence, nor about the authorship of the *Psalms*.

Furthermore, I cannot accept the view that Jesus believed that God was from eternity a Trinity of Father, Son and Holy Spirit. When he was once addressed according to the Gospel record (*Matthew* 19: 16 & 17), as 'Good Master', Jesus replied, "Why call *me* good? Only One is good and that One is God." We would have to conclude that by 'good', Jesus meant 'perfect good' because it seems clear from the record that Jesus saw and acknowledged the capacity for goodness and compassion in many of his fellow human beings. That he would not have seen goodness in the actions of the Samaritan of parable fame, is unthinkable. I believe, however, that he would have understood the source of goodness in human life to be the presence of God's Spirit in human persons. That Jesus himself was a good man is beyond all doubt in my mind.

John records Jesus as stating that 'God is Spirit' (*John* 4: 24), and that accords with the common Jewish understanding of God's presence. When the Psalmist prays (*Psalm* 51: 11), "Take not thy Holy Spirit from me," the tenor of the passage would be as well expressed as, "Depart not from me, O God." Again, when the Psalmist (*Psalm* 139: 7) cries, "Whither shall I go from thy Spirit?" he is saying that God cannot ever be absent from his life. Jesus, when asked on one recorded occasion (*Luke* 10: 25-28) by a scribal student of the Law, what he (the scribe) needed to do to inherit eternal life, answered, "What does it say in the

Law?" The man replied, "Thou shalt love Yahweh thy God with all thy soul, thy strength and thy mind; and thy neighbour as thyself." Jesus responded with the words, "Do this and you will have eternal life." Surely Jesus accepted the Law's testimony, "Hear, O Israel, Yahweh thy God is *One*." If Jesus really understood that God was 'three-in-one' he gave no inkling of that fact.

I have great admiration for, and a considerable understanding of, the process whereby the doctrine of the Trinity evolved and have written further about this in a later chapter. Yet I believe that that doctrine is mistaken and not a part of God's self-revelation, nor a part of Jesus' self-understanding.

CHAPTER 6

St. Paul, the Damascus Road, 'My Gospel', and Jesus

Professor Robert Funk, Chairperson of 'The Jesus Seminar' has stated, "Christianity arose out of the interaction of the historical Jesus and his first companions. It was not invented by Paul. That is the stunning hypothesis of Crossan's *The Birth of Christianity*."[1]

Masterly, and in many ways quite exciting as I found that book to be, I remain as yet unconvinced by its thesis. My own assessment of what seems to me to be the kind of reasonable evidence, quite a bit of it albeit based on speculation, that answers satisfactorily for me the greatest number of knotty problems involved in the issue, leads me still to maintain that the pivotal influence in the formalization of Christian doctrinal claims was indeed that of Paul.

We first hear of Paul, as Saul, in *Acts* 7: 58, on the occasion of the stoning of Stephen, an event to which Saul consented. Some of the pseudepigraphical material presents a very fanatical, anti-Jesus picture of Saul. The Pseudo-Clementine *Recognitions* have him attacking Jesus' brother, James 'the Just', in the Temple some time in the early 40s C.E. The Stephen incident may date from that time also.[2] In one of his post-conversion defence speeches, Paul (Saul) states that he was enlisted by the High Priest of Jerusalem to hound down followers of Jesus, binding men and women alike to bring them back to the city for punishment (*Acts* 22: 4 & 5). Obviously *at that stage* Saul did not think of Jesus as the Christ. But was Jesus being proclaimed as the Christ by anyone at that stage? Stephen who was accused of speaking words against Moses delivered a thoroughly *Moseocentric* defence speech and nowhere in it did he mention the term 'Christ' when speaking of Jesus. He suggested that Jesus was the one of whom Moses said, "A prophet shall the Lord your God raise up from among your brethren, like unto me."[3] That is precisely the same passage that Peter is recorded as citing in reference to Jesus, immediately after calling on the people to repent (*Acts* 3: 19-22), so that God may send the Christ to them, namely, Jesus, whom the heavens must retain until the "restitution of all things", the arrival of the Age to Come. The late Bishop J. A. T. Robinson has concluded that this prediction of Peter indicated that Jesus was not yet the Christ, but at this stage only the Messiah-designate.[4] It seems, therefore, that Jesus is not being testified unequivocally as being the Christ. When I say 'at this stage', my own speculation has the 40s C.E. in mind, but certainly at the time when the Stephen episode was written and when the tradition embodied in Peter's *Acts* 3 speech was composed, where Jesus is seen only to be Messiah-designate according to J. A. T. Robinson and Krister Stendahl. The Stephen passage is peculiar in that the excellent Greek in the prior chapters changes to what the expert French New Testament scholar, Marcel Simon in his detailed study, *St. Stephen and the Hellenists* (1958), calls 'barbarous' Greek. I speculate that the compiler of *The Acts* included this rather poor translation of an earlier Aramaic fragment in the interest of bringing Stephen and hence Saul into the narrative; it also, however, underscores the apparent absence *at that time* of a Christological testimony to Jesus.

We do know for a virtual certainty which reliable extant documents first refer to Jesus as the Christ. They are the letters of Saul, now known to us by his Roman nomenclature, Paul. I believe that the earliest of these are the Thessalonian letters, dated in all probability around 49-50 C.E.[5] So Saul, who in *Acts* 7: 58 would not have dreamed of calling Jesus "Christ", is, as Paul in *2 Thessalonians* 1: 1, openly writing about Jesus Christ. I will have to do some speculating as I try to trace this development in Paul's thinking, but so will everyone else who attempts to fill in the parts of the story! The story of Saul's attack on James in Pseudo-Clementine *Recognitions*, quite probably no less historically reliable than parts of *The Acts*, led not to James' death but to his flight with some of the members of his community of followers of Jesus to somewhere in the Jericho area, which may very well mean somewhere in the neighbourhood of Qumran, the area where the Dead Sea scrolls were found. Jericho itself was about 11 miles (19 kms) from Jerusalem, and Qumran about 9 miles (14 kms) from Jericho. *Acts* 8: 1 refers to "a great persecution against the church at Jerusalem ... and they were scattered abroad throughout the regions of Judea," *not*, mark you well, as far away as Syria, the capital of which, Damascus, was about 150 miles (240 kms) from Jerusalem.

Saul was commissioned by the High Priest of Jerusalem to arrest these followers of Jesus, or 'followers of the Way'. On the way to fulfil his mission he had his 'Damascus Road' experience, arriving at his destination as a man converted to 'the Way.' In reading the account in *Acts* 9 we at first assume that Saul was on his way to Damascus, way north in Syria. It is doubtful whether many or any of Jesus' followers were *there*. Furthermore, Syria was at that time a separate Roman province and not part of Israel. A writ from Jerusalem's High Priest would be unlikely to carry any authority there; it was not under his jurisdiction. Since the *Recognitions*, cited above, reported that James and his Jerusalem followers had fled to an area near Jericho and therefore in the vicinity of Qumran, it is likely that Saul's route led not to a destination 240 kilometres north-east, to Damascus in Syria, but to the area to which the Jerusalem followers of 'the Way' had fled; but why attach the name Damascus to that area? In 1896 Professor Solomon Schechter found, amongst a number of manuscripts in the Cairo Geniza (Egypt), two portions of documents which he later published as *The Zadokite Fragment*.[6] They were addressed to "those entering the new covenant in *the land of Damascus*,"[7] and have become known as *The Damascus Document*. The community at Qumran understood themselves to be a community of 'the new covenant', and when manuscript fragments containing the same material as Schechter's *Zadokite Fragments* were found in Cave 4 at Qumran (4Q 266-272), it becomes apparent that *that* area must, at the time of the Cairo documents' writing, have been known as 'the land of Damascus'. Saul, then, was on his way to that area when he was struck by an intense flash of light and rendered blind. In this state he testifies that he was spoken to by Jesus and given instructions as to what he should do, now that the direction of his life had radically changed.

What Paul did in the next years is somewhat confusing. In his own version of the sequence of events recorded in his letter to the Galatians, he states that after his meeting with Jesus, he did not "confer with any other persons, nor did I go up to Jerusalem, I went into Arabia and returned again to 'Damascus', (*Galatians* 1: 16 & 17). Then after three years I went up to Jerusalem ... " These words would have been written well over a decade before the publication of the narrative in *Acts*, where he stays a while in Damascus, preaching the message that Jesus was the Christ. Some Jews there planned to kill him but 'the disciples' helped him to escape and he went then to Jerusalem. After preaching there for a while Paul was again threatened with death but 'the brethren' brought him to Caesarea on the coast and then dispatched him to the city of his birth, Tarsus in Asia Minor. The *Galatians* account is likely to be the more accurate. My speculation is that he went to Qumran where James and the others of the followers of 'the Way' had fled and from there went further south into the desert to think through the great change that had occurred in his life. He later went back to Qumran where he would have taken a lively interest in the kind of Scriptural interpretation which was being practised there; a search for the meaning of the ancient texts as they applied to the current situation in Palestine, an interpretation known as the 'pesher' of the text. I believe that it was in this context that Paul came to assert that Jesus was the Christ and that God had raised him from the dead and the resurrection had thus begun. I imagine Paul's thinking may well have been along lines such as: 'I was in Jerusalem when Jesus was executed but on my way to finding followers of this man, I myself was confronted by him. He spoke to me and I asked him who he was and he said he was Jesus' (*Acts* 9: 1-5). Thus for Paul, Jesus whom he knew had been killed was in fact alive again. From this fact Paul, an apocalyptically minded Pharisaical Jew, came to assert that the resurrection had begun and 'the age to come' had been inaugurated by Jesus, the Christ. I believe Paul was the first person to come to these conclusions for the reasons I have just set out.

Paul, however, would have had to see a real problem here, for if Jesus was the Christ, why had God allowed him to be crucified? To answer this, Paul engaged in his own Scriptural 'pesher' interpretation of passages such as *Isaiah* 53, to demonstrate its fulfilment in the death of God's own Son, the Messiah, who "was despised and rejected of men ... was wounded for our transgressions ... on whom Yahweh laid the iniquity of us all." Thus, I suggest, speculate, and believe, Paul's doctrine of the atonement for human sin through the death of Jesus emerged and was promulgated in what Paul called '*my* gospel' (*Romans* 2: 16; 16: 25). I believe this 'messianic' interpretation roused the displeasure of the Qumran community and Paul departed from them to follow his own mission.[8] The 'Suffering Servant' of *Isaiah* 53 was not considered a royal, kingly figure, a messianic figure. His role in *Isaiah* was expounded centuries before the apocalyptic notion of *the* Messiah was emerging, and *that* figure was certainly not one who would suffer, but one who would inaugurate 'The Age to Come'. There is a tradition in Judaism of the 'just men', the *Lamed-Vovniks*, humble God-chosen persons whose lives follow the pattern of Isaiah's 'suffering servant'. In his tender, compelling novel *The Last of the Just*, André Schwarz-Bart puts on the lips of a major character, Mordecai, these words: "The Lamed-Vovnik takes our suffering upon himself, and he raises it to heaven and sets it at the feet of the Lord – who forgives. Which is why the world goes on ... in spite of all our sins." [9]

Jesus, the Jew, knew of and trusted in the atonement, the reconciliation that flows from God's eternal and unfathomable acts of forgiveness. I do not believe that he ever presumed that it would be by his death that a once-for-all atonement for the sins of the world would be achieved, though he may well have been viewed by those around him as one of the 'just'. In that tradition the 'just persons' did not recognize themselves as such. No, it was Paul's 'gospel' that proclaimed that the death of Jesus, the Christ, was God's planned-from-eternity propitiation for the sins of all humankind. This 'gospel' held a great attraction for Gentiles where its converting power produced manifest results in Paul's missionary work as it has also in the evangelistic work of the Christian churches ever since. I believe it also gave a great boost to the triumphalistic view of Jesus' death as a victory over sin and death. I hold the view that Paul, in his recorded meetings with certain of the apostles, convinced them of the worldwide possibilities of success in proclaiming this message in their preaching and epistle and gospel writing. Certainly the Petrine and Johannine branches of primitive Christianity adopted this view.[10] But was it an integral part of Jesus' message? I think not. Mark states (1: 14) that "Jesus came into Galilee, preaching the gospel of *God*" (RSV). The KJV translated from late manuscripts reads "preaching the gospel of the kingdom of God." John Dominic Crossan insists that Jesus did not say "I bring you the kingdom", but that it was present and open to all, unmediated or, as Crossan puts it, "unbrokered".[11] When Jesus sent out his disciples in pairs to announce throughout the small hamlets in Galilee the *presence* of God's kingdom, they had joyful success.[12] God's forgiveness available to the disciples' hearers only through Jesus' mediating efficacy, and in particular through his death on the Cross, was *not* a part of the disciples' message. Crossan maintains that this was *not* a 'Jesus Movement', but a Kingdom of God Movement. I conclude that although the major element of Paul's 'gospel' came to be written into the record of the four Gospels, they were not part of the gospel of God which Jesus proclaimed.[13]

CHAPTER 7

With Respect To 'God'

God is the central reality of my faith. I believe the same was true for Jesus. Yet I do not hold the views about God which seem to be generally accepted by most persons of faith. The 'heresy' that has brought me stronger criticism than any other is in reference to the doctrine of creation. The creeds declare that God is "the maker of heaven and earth, and of all things visible and invisible." In my experience, almost all persons of faith claim that God is the creator of the physical universe – that vast mystery embracing millions of galaxies, including stars which are billions of light years distant from our planet. The terms used by astrophysicists are quite beyond the wildest imaginations of most of us. In his stimulating book *Is Jesus God?*[1] Michael Morwood cites the fact that a thimble-full of matter from a neutron star would weigh a hundred million tonnes on our planet. He further points out that our sun, one of the millions of stars in our galaxy, "converts 600 million tonnes of hydrogen into helium every second, and has been doing so for four billion years!" All this in a universe which expands by more than a million kilometres every hour! Now, Morwood, along with almost all people of faith with whom I've had conversations, believes that God is the creator of this unthinkably vast universe.

CHAPTER 7

Now, I believe that God is *present* in the natural world. I cannot *know* that such is true for the astronomically vast entities described above, although I wouldn't rule it out. Yet I do *not* believe that the Reality I worship as God, whom I know, love and trust, whose presence I experience in my daily life, was and is the creator of all nature. I remember hearing the celebrated physicist, Professor Paul Davies, say in a radio interview that while he did not subscribe to the Christian view of a personal God, yet he found the natural physical world functioning in many ways with such a degree of observable intelligence, that he could not write off the notion that behind the evolution of the universe there seemed to be an amazingly intelligent mind; a mathematical mind, I believe he suggested. I know so little about such things but Davies' point of view may well be right.

Yet I do not equate such a mathematical mind with the Reality whose Presence is central to my faith and whom I find I cannot believe to be the creator, sustainer and controller of this wondrous universe of which we are a part. The Bible certainly asserts, and Jesus, it seems to me, clearly did believe, that God was the creator of heaven and earth. Why then do I reject that belief as part of my faith? A leading British atheist/scholar and evolutionary biologist Richard Dawkins has written somewhere, "Nature is *never cruel*. It is totally *indifferent*, disinterested." I believe this to be true.

On Boxing Day, December 26, 2004, a *tsunami* in South East Asia caused the death of thousands of men, women and innocent little children and the total destruction of millions of dollars worth of properties. It simply happened; nature was following its evolutionary course. Meteorologists may be able partly to explain how, and in a narrow sense, why it occurred. In no way, however, did nature *intend* such disastrous destruction. We do not blame or hold nature morally accountable for such an event. God did not and, I believe, *could not* stop it happening. While nature, then, is never cruel but indifferent as to how it plays itself out in the universe according to whatever 'laws' there may be, I believe that God also is *never cruel* but in contrast to nature, is *never indifferent*, but is totally *compassionate*, present with and concerned for all who suffer horrific agonies and death from all such natural disasters, large and small, which occur in this world. Where was God in that *tsunami* disaster? I believe God was present with all the suffering and *known* to be present to many who opened their sorrowful hearts to God in the midst of the tragic circumstances. God, who is "pure universal Love", is the One who urges believers and unbelievers alike to respond with compassion, love and generosity towards those who have suffered in all natural disasters. Mark you well, not all disastrous events are due to the indifference of nature's evolutionary occurrences. Many are due to the human lust for power, to human greed, to human careless and irresponsible living, to alienation between nation and nation, between the powerful and the weak and defenceless, between the rich and the poor; in short, to human *sin*, that is, alienation (see my words about sin in Chapter 2).

Many of my conversation partners in these matters still maintain that God is ultimately in control of this universe and of human history, but that God will not intervene on account of God's insistence on giving humankind 'freedom of will'. I am not impressed by this argument. Earthquakes; many (but not all) floods; raging fires caused by lightning or spontaneous combustion; the existence of many viruses and germs and the seemingly random mutations which sometimes occur in human bodies; *these have nothing to do with the freedom of the human will.* They are just part of the process of the evolution of this universe, of our planet.

I am asserting that our psycho-somatic entities, our body-mind continua, are the 'gift', if you will, of the amoral evolutionary process. Our minds are a function of our brains which are a part of our biological make-up. Now, I believe that into this situation God has breathed the wonderfully mysterious gift of the Spirit of Love and Justice. God's Presence (and I capitalize the word purposely) is not part of the evolutionary process, in my view, but a gift of God's grace: God's Spirit inhabits the physical, body-mind world. George Fox, the founder of The Society of Friends (Quakers), asserted that there is "that of God" in every person, and, I am inclined to add, in every living thing. If we nurture, attend to 'that of God' within us: if we live following the way of love, of compassion, of justice, many of the human tragedies and disasters in the personal, social, national and international spheres of life would not occur. God does respect our freedom to choose to follow the way of compassion, justice and peace. Humankind's record of rejecting God's way of love and justice is writ large on history's pages.

The question often asked of me in conversations is this: if God is not the creator, sustainer and controller of the natural universe, then who was/is? And when? Clearly we are speaking of billions of light-years in the so-called past. Davies' suggestion of a fantastic mathematical 'mind' cannot be ruled out. Yet must the universe have had a creator?

Traditionally, that is, according to the orthodoxy of a number of living religions such as Judaism, Islam, and Christianity, God is an *uncreated* Reality. To what I have often referred as the Grade 1 question, "Who made God?", the answer has been, "God has just always been from eternity, uncreated, self-existing." If people can live with that explanation with regard to God, why not also with the existence of the natural cosmos? It simply *is* there and always has been. I know that 'always' is an adverb relating to time. We do not have a ready vocabulary with regard to eternity. I can live with that.

I believe that God cannot be *defined*; all attempts to do so are inadequate. When I am asked how I describe or talk about God, many phrases and epithets come to mind. I do *not* think of omnipotence (all-powerful), though *love* is a most powerful force of influence; nor do I think of omniscience (knowing everything), though I believe God knows me (see *Psalm* 139), and that I know God. I like the line of poet/hymn-writer George Rawson which speaks of God as "Mystery of Love Adored."[2] I like the simple epithet, The Presence. I speak of 'The Holy One'; the awareness of the sacred dimension in life. I refer to God as 'the Holy Spirit of Love and Justice'. The categories that centre on God are such as love, compassion, wonder, awe, *joy*, as opposed to happiness, for 'happiness *happens* but joy abides.' I experience God in the *recognition* of beauty and the sense of significance which I sense in many of my activities and relationships.

Paul Tillich once said (in class) in his deep guttural tones, "God is *not* a person, but God is intensely *personal*." I find this very meaningful. It is the personal aspect of God that enables us to have intimate communion with God. In short, I put my trust in a personal God, the 'Inward Teacher' whose promptings I attend to,[3] whom, in a deep way, I sense to be present in my life though I cannot prove this to be true by logical argument. In fact I believe that all the so-called philosophical arguments for God's existence are logically flawed, though those of Professor John Finnis are highly attractive to my mind. The writer of *Psalm* 139, however, had no need of argument to support his warm and vital testimony to God's presence in his life. His testimony has 'rung true' for millions of persons throughout the ages, as it does for me today.

The ancient Hebrew record (*Genesis* 2: 7) speaks of God forming Adam (Hebrew for 'humankind') and breathing God's spirit or breath into him, and he became a 'living' soul or person (in Hebrew: *nephesh*). Now, a *nephesh* is not an inanimate clay model, but a 'soul', a 'person', a body and mind entity. The qualifier 'living' in 'living *nephesh*' refers, I believe, not to biological life but to the eternal Spirit of God in humankind. Certainly the ancient Hebrews believed God had created the biological body-mind *nephesh*, person or soul. They had no scientific knowledge of physical and biological evolution. Yet they did believe, as the later writer of *Ecclesiastes* stated, that 'God has set eternity in our hearts' (3: 11). I believe that God's Spirit within our bodies and minds can and does influence us in wonderfully healing ways.

Trinitarians often seek to show the reasonableness of the 'Three-in-One' doctrine by use of analogies drawn from everyday life. We see the sun as an object in the sky; we see its rays of sunshine all around us which not only warm us but promote growth in plant life. All three of these aspects constitute one reality. Likewise, ice, water and steam are all manifestations of hydrogen oxide. Such analogies in no way prove the proposition that God is Three Persons in One God, but if that doctrine is accepted as the truth about God, they may help many Christians to have some understanding of the mystery of the Trinity. I, too, have a simple analogy which may help in understanding my assertion that though God is present in the world of nature, God is distinguishable from the natural universe and not its creator, sustainer, and controller. Imagine a raw sponge, off-white or light beige in its natural coloration. This sponge can be coloured with a deep blue dye which renders it a blue sponge. The colour is all of a piece with the sponge. If we immerse it in water it remains a blue sponge, usable for washing things. It is clear, however, that the water is not the sponge itself, yet it is fully present in the sponge. Although no analogy is really adequate, I liken God's presence in the natural universe and especially in human life to the water in the sponge. I repeat that I believe God's presence is not part of our evolutionary inheritance but the gift of God's gracious Spirit. Following the recent *tsunami* disaster I heard and read many expressions of the view that we could clearly no longer believe that God was a loving, compassionate Reality. That saddened me greatly. Yet when the generally accepted understanding of God, taught to many of us from early childhood, is that God is the maker and controller of all there is, it is understandable that some, perhaps many, will draw such a conclusion. My experience of God as testified to in this chapter makes such a conclusion very much mistaken.

CHAPTER 7

One reader of the draft manuscript of this book, the Revd Dr. John Bodycomb (see the Dedication page and the opening part of Chapter 2), has suggested that I have not taken enough notice of, done justice to, the work of a group of eminent scientists in the areas of nuclear- and astrophysics; some of them priests or persons of strong comparatively orthodox faith, with regard to their account of creation. For the sake of further completeness, I wish to address briefly this issue. I am taking the Revd Professor Arthur R. Peacocke[4] as a major representative of this group (see the Endnotes for examples of his writings from which the following description of the process, as far as I can understand it, comes. At the outset, however, let me testify to the deep sense of admiration, indeed of thrill, that I experience in reading his account of the God of Creation. His erudition is awesome.

God, an uncreated Reality at the genesis of Peacocke's magnificent manifesto, was 'All-that-Was', but took the risk of calling into being within Godself, the 'Other', a field of 'vibrating energy' which had the potential, following the immutable regulations or laws with which God had endowed its processes, to explode, thus forming the universe and creating 'space'. All this occurred about a dozen or more billion years ago. Creation ever more and more complex continued (and continues) to burst forth, bringing into existence on its procession the evolution of all living entities including the gradual emergence of humankind.

Nature follows its 'divinely established regularities' allowing its inherent properties free rein to be and to become. These processes once brought into existence cannot be altered by the Creator 'breaking in' to the system, for that would be inconsistent with God's very nature in deciding to take the risk to thus limit Godself's omnipotence and omniscience. God is omnipotent and omniscient (all-powerful and all-knowing) only in so far as it is logically possible, that is, not inconsistent with God's original decision and plan for creation, to be so. God, although giving existence to each instance of 'becoming' is not able to *know* what the future holds for the universe. With these self-assumed limitations imposing themselves, God suffers 'with, in, and under' the natural processes. God is a Being of 'unfathomable richness, including and penetrating all-that-is' but is not exhausted by it. That is to say that Peacocke's position is not 'pantheistic' (God is the whole universe, period), but 'pan-en-theistic' (present within the whole universe but without such a definition exhausting the significance of God). He (A. R. Peacocke) thus dynamically blends or transcends the popularly-believed dichotomy of 'matter v. spirit'. In God's creative energy both law (necessity) and chance are present. We have often thought of chance as destroying all purpose and reliability of meaning. Chance alone would likely produce chaos, while law alone would prove static, undynamic.

The assertion of the role of chance in Darwinism thus introduces the blend of chance and law. Evolution thus becomes, in Peacocke's words, the 'disguised friend of faith', the title of one of his books as listed in the Endnotes. While science alone cannot give an answer to the question, 'Why is there anything?', Peacocke's faith assertion of the One who at the beginning was 'All-that-Was' and who called forth and endowed the potential of 'the Other', does, for those who accept that assertion and its consequent unfolding, answer that question. Affirming that this, his understanding of God's relationship to the natural order of the universe, is *not* a *proof* of God as Ultimate Reality, he nevertheless puts it forward as the best explanation there is. I am *not* so convinced. My reason for saying this does not, I believe, stem from the deficiences in my scientific knowledge. In spite of its enormous attractiveness, Peacocke's understanding of God as the sole, absolute prime-mover in the creation of the evolutionary processes still – the risk-taking and self-imposed limitations notwithstanding – leaves God, in the last analysis, as responsible and indeed accountable for the disasters and suffering brought about by these so-called divinely regulated processes. A creator who *chose* to risk such chances is responsible for such a *choice*. I find such a conclusion inescapable.

Better, in my limited view, is the explanation I proposed earlier in this chapter with nature not the creation of God, 'never cruel but quite disinterested' (Dawkins), not culpable for the outcome of its processes even though some of these seem to show evidence of an intelligence working within them. This view certainly keeps alive the dichotomy of two uncreated, self-existing 'powers', so to speak: the natural world and God present within this world with all Love's powers but not accountable for nature's processes. Our 'body-mind' entities which are our evolutionary heritage can be responsible for cruelties and disasters when we, individually or corporately, choose not to attend to the urgings, wooings and promptings of 'that of God' in us. Greed and hatred are evidence of 'the naked ape' aspect of our evolutionary-driven natures, but these occur through *our own choices*. Acts of love, compassion and self-sacrifice are evidence of the presence of 'the mystery of love adored' recognized or unrecognized in our lives. That God is present in all the suffering of humankind and, indeed, of all living things, is a truth I deeply believe. For God to be, in the last analysis (the bottom line) *responsible* for setting in motion the natural processes which cause such suffering is an unacceptable proposition from my admittedly limited point of view. For this reason I do not believe that God is the creator, sustainer of the physical universe.

Before concluding this chapter about God, I wish to make an excursus on the question of the doctrine of the Trinity. It will be abundantly clear to those who have read this book's previous chapters that I am not committed to a belief in this doctrine, yet I still find it fascinating to read and to ponder deeply on books and articles on this issue. It is a central teaching of orthodox Christian belief about the nature of God. Some writers insist that if God is Love there is a relationality within Godself, a kind of community within the Godhead. The deep spirituality displayed, for example, in many of the Psalmists' reflections on God's presence in their lives, however, seems not to necessitate or even suggest a Triune God. If Jesus believed himself to be the incarnation of the Second Person of the Trinity, he seems to give no inkling of that fact in his teaching about God. Holy Spirit, as referred to in the Hebrew Scriptures is a wonderful way of speaking about Godself and not a separate though inseparable 'Person' within the nature of God.

British theologian, the late Principal Nathanael Micklem, writing as 'Ilico' in *The British Weekly*[5] asks whether, "had we not received this doctrine from antiquity, and were we to attempt to speak of the nature of God in terms natural to us, would we have ever hit upon a Trinitarian formulation?"

CHAPTER 7

I think not. He also asks whether we would be "disloyal to Scripture if we spoke of God known to us as Father, as Wisdom, as Word, and as Holy Spirit? Would a Quaternity (rather than a Trinity) of this sort involve a change in our religious faith?" Such questions as these are indeed engaging, even if we are believers in the doctrine of the Trinity.

John Dominic Crossan said in a seminar which I chaired that essentially all religions are small 't' trinitarian. There is a central reality; those who make that reality's essence known in humankind's history; and the communities of faith and practice who follow and embody the spirit of this knowledge, faith and practice in their worship and daily living. For Jews the central reality is Yahweh (Adonai), Moses and the prophets spell out the implications of Yahweh's intentions for their living, the spirit of which is practised in synagogue attendance and High Holy Days rituals. Yet no practising Jews would ever consider themselves Trinitarians! With Islam we could well consider a 'Quaternity' (à la 'Ilico' above); Allah; Muhammad; the Koran; and the daily prayer schedules. Crossan's notion is interesting but a far cry from the Christian doctrine of God as the Three-in-One and the One-in-Three. The doctrine of the Trinity is uniquely Christian, and if true, makes a claim for Christianity as the one faith that rightly understands the nature of God, does it not? I find *that* divisive and unproductive with regard to what I believe is the faithful following of the way of Jesus, who was himself a faithful Jew who insisted that God alone (whom he called 'Father' – a relational rather than a gender epithet) should be worshipped.

CHAPTER 8

Tying Up Some Loose Ends

There are still some issues about which I am often questioned and which I'd like to address in this 'testimony'. Here I may be less of a heretic!

CONCERNING PRAYER

Prayer for me is not so much a matter of 'saying my prayers' as of "attending to the promptings of the Inward Teacher," to use the words of Quaker, Dr. Paul Lacey of Philadelphia. I am slowly learning to 'practise the Presence of God' day by day, hour by hour. One aid to this I found in a novel by Elizabeth Goudge, *The Scent of Water*,[1] in which an ageing priest says to a troubled woman, one of the book's main characters, "There are essentially only three prayers and each has three words," and I cite from memory: "Thee I adore"; "God, have mercy"; and "Into Thy hands". I have for years used these small utterances, all from the *Psalms*, as 'mantras' to help me focus on the Inner Light. Often I am asked about the efficacy of so-called 'intercessory' prayer and whether my practice of prayer includes intercession. I spend time each day centering down into an awareness of God's presence with me; then I try to visualize those persons or situations for whom I have a special concern. I focus on the realization that God's Presence is there with those persons and in those situations and I concentratedly "wrap them around with Light and Love," and trust that they will have a growing awareness of being held 'in the Light'. The mantra 'Into Thy Hands' is a wonderful focus for such intercessions. I rarely make any 'requests' in such a practice of prayer other than trusting that the presence and the peace of God is being realized in those persons and situations.

LIFE AFTER DEATH

I happen to be a strong believer in personal existence in the realm of the Spirit after physical death, yet it is not an issue of any major importance in my life of faith. If there is no such life after death, no persons who have died will feel cheated or feel that they have had their hopes dashed. I don't believe in it because it would be unfair for all whose earthly lives have been filled with untold misery, injustice or suffering not to have some kind of reparation or fulfilment in 'the next life'. I do not believe in rewards or punishments in some kind of future existence after death. I do not believe in it because Jesus did so believe; and he *did*. What then leads me to be convinced of this belief? A number of things, and I will begin with what I have every reason to believe was a true story.

A Canadian journalist (I believe his name was Kirke, but my memory may well be at fault, but no matter) used to motor around small towns and villages in a 1928 (or so) Essex or Hupmobile, interviewing people. I believe his TV show of ½ hour duration was called "Our Town" or some such name. I watched in the 1980s and '90s many times and taped episodes. One morning he was in a mining town in

Nova Scotia, standing near to the mine talking to the mine's manager. He said he'd heard that the manager had had a very scary experience some years previously. The manager related the story. He had come down from his home on a small rise near where they were standing. It was a Sunday morning and as was his habit, he wanted just to check everything out in preparation for the coming week's work. As he was approaching the mine entrance his mother shouted to him from the house, "John! Stop right there!" Wondering what the problem was, he stopped and turned to look up at his house. He chuckled, because he realised that his mother had died some six years previously. He turned to go on, but before he had taken one step, there was a huge explosion and the mine blew up.

The manager told Kirke that he had not been thinking about his mother; that he was not a religious man nor given to any strong belief about life after death. The incident left him somewhat shaken and wondering. He'd had no premonition of any such disaster. The mine had been considered a very safe one for years. I saw and heard the interview. It seemed to me that the manager felt convinced that it was his mother who had gotten through to him and that her intervention had saved his life, in all probability. There may be many reasons why the manager should have stopped suddenly when he did: some faint smell of a gas, something far back in his mind that gave him the feeling that all was not right at the mine. I want to emphasize that this story is *not* a major reason why I find belief in life after death quite reasonable. Yet it is an incident with no religious nuances which supports that belief. The unexpectedness of the explosion and the fact that it occurred straight after what he recognized immediately was his mother's shout requires some explanation.

More convincing for me is the frequent experience I have of sensing a 'guardian angel' in my own life. I often feel a bit shy speaking of this but when I do, I frequently find the hearers of many different levels of attainment saying that they have the same sense of being strangely guided or kept from foolish actions by what seems to them to be a spiritual presence manifesting itself. I also remember an ageing maiden aunt of mine on her death-bed and right at the moment of dying, opening her eyes and, with a smile, simply saying what seemed like a deeply contented 'Oh! Oh!'

My most compelling reason for my belief in personal existence after death arises from my deep experiences of the presence of God in my present life. I have a deep sense of communing with God in what seems to me the same way that many of the writers of the *Psalms*, Jesus himself, Brother Lawrence (of the kitchen), Mother Julian, and countless thousands of ordinary folk like myself have testified to. Now, when I die, God will not cease to exist and therefore the spiritual relationship I have had with God in this life will, I believe, continue.

None of this may be at all convincing to many readers, but then again, to some it may ring a bell of authenticity. Suffice it to say again that belief in life after death is a very natural part of my faith experience, but not one of major importance.

WITH REGARD TO THE BIBLE

Understanding and interpreting the Bible has been my life's

work since I was inducted into my first parish church in 1954. It is obviously an important factor in my pilgrimage of faith. It is salutary, however, to remember that great communities of faith in Old Testament times had no Bible to guide them – no documents at all – but only stories to rehearse. Likewise, the early Christian communities thrived well without a New Testament to guide them. In the faith of many folk today the Bible is seemingly almost as central as God's very self; for Billy Graham, for example, the words, "the Bible says" render all argument unnecessary. This is because the Bible is understood by them to be the inerrant Word of God.

In one of his Princeton Lectures (1962) which I attended, Karl Barth stated that the Bible was *not* the Word of God but rather a *testimony*, or more accurately, many testimonies, to the Word of God. God's *Word* in Biblical terms is in effect a way of speaking about God's self, God's creative energy of Love in relationship to humankind: God's purposes and intentions for human living. Many preachers introduce their reading of the Scriptures with the words, "Hear the Word of God as written in ..." I learned quite early to say, "Listen for a word from God as I read from the Scriptures", or from the writings of a poet or a novelist.

On one occasion as I conducted my lunch-hour sessions, "A Theologian on the Hot-Seat", a student addressed me thus: "You are the professor of Biblical Studies in this university, yet you are frequently 'poking holes' through the Bible when I believe you should be upholding it." I suppose 'poking holes' is a colloquialism for 'criticising', and I replied, "Yes, I am a critical Biblical scholar and that is what my profession and ministerial calling require me to be. For a considerable number of testimonies in the Bible to what the writers believed at the time of writing to be the will of God, seem to me clearly to be contrary to the nature of God, 'the Mystery of Love Adored'. Did God really desire the killing of all the men, women and children in Jericho, as carried out by Joshua (the Old Testament 'Jesus')? I say thee nay!

There are dozens of other passages which likewise describe incidents or make assertions which I believe most thinking people would not accept as truly reflecting the mind of God, nor worthily receiving God's favourable endorsement. Even the *Psalms* which contain many of the most inspirational words through which millions of folk throughout the ages have heard the authentic voice of God, both in blessing and in judgement, nevertheless also contain passages of hatred and horror which reflect the human bigotries of the writers and not the mind of God, or so I believe and assert.

Furthermore, a careful critical approach to Biblical studies is necessary in the area of responsible interpretation of the Scriptural text. A lack of knowledge of the original languages in which the Bible was written; and a lack of an honest assessment of the context, the historical milieu in which the Biblical text was formed, can lead to wrong-headed interpretations. I give a clear example of this with respect to the widely promulgated, but patently erroneous understanding of Job's words "I know that my redeemer liveth ..." (*Job* 19: 25 & 26) in Appendix 'A', which follows this chapter. In earlier chapters I have discussed the provenance of the terms '*the* Christ' and '*the* resurrection of the dead' in the centuries just prior to the Common Era, the times in which Jesus lived and died. I have pointed out the intricate anomalies regarding the understanding of these terms as found in the New Testament record (see again Chapters 3 and 4). An honest rigorous assessment of the evidence for the truth of these various viewpoints requires a critical approach to the Biblical passages concerned and a willingness to change one's mind on such issues if more accurate *evidence* is educed, developed from reliable available data.

In sum, I believe it is inappropriate and misleading to regard the Bible as inerrant. This gives a collection of *books* virtually the status of God, which is a form of idolatry. Yet the Bible is a remarkable book and my critical approach to it has strengthened, not lessened, the influence of its message on my day to day living. How can we know which influences stemming from our reading and study of the Bible are authentically tuned to the mind of God? I believe that there is no sure way appropriate to every person's faith. Tillich once said in a class lecture, "All faith contains doubt!" and he added these words from *Mark* 9: 24: "Lord, I believe; help thou my unbelief." I believe the evidence I have adduced in support of what I have written in this book is strong, and for the unconvinced, make sure your reasons are honest and equally as strong.

Here endeth my testimony.

APPENDIX 'A'

Article by Paul Trudinger
published in *The Downside Review*, Vol. 124, No. 436,
July 2006.

"I Know That My Redeemer Liveth"
A Note on *Job* 19: 25 & 26.

Job 19: 25 & 26 in the King James Version, reads as follows:

> I know that my redeemer liveth,
> and that he shall stand at the latter day upon the earth.
> And though ... worms destroy this body,
> Yet in my flesh shall I see God.

I'd be willing to wager that these words spoken by Job as rendered in the memorable phrasing of the KJV would not be nearly so well known by so many people, both 'churched' and 'unchurched', if it were not for their occurrence as a much-loved soprano aria in G. F. Handel's *Messiah*. *In the context of this oratorio*, these words along with the tenor aria, "But Thou didst not leave his soul in hell, nor didst Thou suffer Thy Holy One to see corruption" (*Psalm* 16: 10, with a *significant* pronominal adjustment!), are confidently assumed to carry a proleptic reference to life beyond the grave, and in particular, a prediction of Jesus' triumph over death by his resurrection. Other translations seem also to imply an eschatological reference in these words. Msgr Ronald Knox's translation from the Latin Vulgate reads thus:

> This at least I know, that one lives on who will vindicate me,
> rising up from the dust *when the last day comes*.
> Once more my skin shall clothe me,
> And in my flesh I shall have sight of God.[1]

And when Professor Samuel Terrien of Yale declares in his commentary that these words are the *most momentous* expression of faith which may be found in the poem, and *perhaps in the entire*

Hebrew Bible,² (italics mine), it would appear that he is stating that here Job is testifying to something quite out of the ordinary. I think not.

I would insist that we should see the words in the context of our understanding of the purpose of the book of Job as a whole. As far as an expression of Job's faith as such is concerned, I doubt that we could find a stronger testimony than his words, "Though he slay me, yet will I trust in him" (13: 15, KJV). Professor W. A. Irwin calls our text, "One of the great enunciations of the Dialogues."³ That it surely is and most importantly so because it points to, moves the dialogue in the direction of, the fulfilment of the book's purpose, my understanding of which I will shortly set forth. From the outset of his troubles, when his wife upbraids him with the words, "Why do you still hold fast to your integrity? Curse God and die!" Job defends God in the face of all his woes: "Shall we receive good at the hand of God, and shall we not receive evil?" (2: 9 & 10)

Then throughout thirty or more chapters in which Job's so-called comforters, Eliphaz, Bildad, and Zophar heap argument upon argument, reason upon reason, trying to convince Job that all his troubles are punishments deserved on account of his or his family's sins, Job maintains his innocence before God: "Far be it from me to say that you are right; till I die I will not put away my integrity from me" (Ch. 27: 5, RSV), and further, "I hold unflinchingly to my innocence; not for one hour need I reproach myself" (27: 6, Moffatt). We speak sometimes of 'the patience of Job', but in these chapters he comes across as very *impatient* with those *who will not let him be patient* and await for his vindication by God which, he affirms in the words of our text, will eventually ("at the latter day" – i.e. in a later time) be forthcoming. But that cannot be "though worms shall have destroyed this body," i.e. after he has died. For Job has earlier in the story declared categorically that he does not believe in a life after death. In Chapter 14: 7 and 10-12, he avers:

> There is hope for a tree that is felled; it may flourish yet again, the shoots of it need not fail ... But man dies and is laid low; he breathes his last and where is he? ... as a river wastes away and dries up, so man lies down and *rises not again*.

Our text, however, has Job asserting that, "In my flesh (that is, while I am still alive) I shall see God." He *does* see God (*Job* 42: 5), and it must needs be so, for this accords, as we shall see, with the book's purpose.

It seems to be commonly held that the book is about the problem of suffering. This is what I've usually been told by young theological students when I've asked them what they think *Job* is all about. Archibald MacLeish takes that position in his famous play, *J.B.*[4] But does the story attempt any real convincing answer to this problem? Clearly, no. For when the story comes to its climax in the last five chapters where God meets with Job and addresses him, 'the storehouses of the snow', 'the cords of Orion', 'the freedom of the wild ass', 'the egg hatching practices of the ostrich,' 'the breeding habits of wild mountain goats'; all these and much more are spoken of by God, but nary a word about suffering; the problem of suffering in general nor Job's suffering in particular. In a most insightful article Professor Henry McKeating suggests that "the central issue of the book of Job" concerns not the problem of suffering but the question, "How can we go on *believing in God*?"[5] The story's answer is not one to satisfy the philosopher, but for Job the very question is rendered pointless; it is completely by-passed. In awe Job confesses, "I have been uttering things I did not understand, things too wonderful for me, which I did not know" (Ch. 42: 3); he can but "repent in dust and ashes". In meeting with God Job has been deeply humbled, where humility was not a very noticeable trait in the earlier dialogues, but as McKeating points out, he has *not* been humiliated. His conviction strongly asserted in our text has been fulfilled: "I had heard of thee by the hearing of the ear, but *now my eye seeth thee*" (42: 5). It has been said by some commentators that in all the words God spoke He did not unequivocally 'vindicate' Job's stance. Perhaps not directly, but in strongly opposing the behaviours of the three 'comforters' He does in a sense champion Job's cause, as Norman Habel suggests.[6] For God says to those three 'friends', "You have not spoken of me what is right, as my servant Job has" (42: 7).[7]

So to the 'bottom line'. How are we to construe the words of our text, *Job* 19: 25 & 26, in a way in keeping with the tenor of the 'central issue' of the book? The first two lines of the quatrain, v. 25a & b, and the fourth line, v. 26b, can stand as they are in the Hebrew text. The third line, v. 26a, is agreed upon by virtually all scholars of the Hebrew text to be totally confusing. Irwin, cited above, calls it "obscure and completely irrational."[8] You will note that in my citation, at the heading of this piece, of the KJV translation used in the Handel aria, I omitted three words. The line in the KJV reads: "And *though* after my skin *worms* destroy this body;" but this is worse than awkward. The words 'my skin' (Heb. *'ori*) do occur in the Hebrew text but the word used in four or five places in Job for 'worm' (Heb. *rimmah*) does not appear in the text in 19: 26. All translations, therefore, contain speculations. I think the United Bible Society's *Good News Bible: Today's English Version* is fairly much in keeping with the 'mood' of the text. It reads:

> But I know there is someone in heaven
> who will come at last to my defence.
> Even after my skin is eaten away by disease, (which it was!)
> while still in this body I will see God.[9]

Or possibly line 3, v. 26a, was a rhetorical question put by Job who was quite dissatisfied with the point of view put to him that if he is indeed innocent he will *ultimately* be vindicated (by history?). He impatiently cries out:

> I *know* that my vindicator will appear on earth some time
> in the future; but when? when my body has been destroyed
> in death? (That's no help to me in my present situation)
> I am determined to have my day in court with God while
> I'm still alive, 'in my flesh'.

Whatever the speculated version of v. 26a may be, the text as a whole cannot be construed, I believe, rightfully to bear a meaning appropriable for the libretto of the aria in *Messiah!* Pity. That soprano aria still tugs at my heart-strings!

APPENDIX 'B'

Article by Paul Trudinger
published in *Faith and Freedom*, Vol. 54, Part 1, pp. 34-45.

The Gospels as Pauline Christology Historicized

A Speculation *Revisted*

Professor John Dominic Crossan has given it as his opinion that many of the details concerning Jesus which are asserted in the Gospels, especially those relating to his birth and death, are not historical events remembered, but rather they are Hebrew Scriptural prophecies historicized.[1] Other scholars have made a similar claim. Bishop J. S. Spong has averred both in a chapter on Judas Iscariot in *Liberating the Gospels*[2] and even more forcibly in a Public Lecture entitled, 'Judas Iscariot: A Personification of a Christian Prejudice' at the Vancouver School of Theology[3] that all the details concerning Judas which appear in the Gospels are traceable to Scripture passages and are in fact veiled references to Judah or the Jewish people who 'betrayed' Jesus in that they did not accept him as their Messiah. They are personified, according to Spong's view, in Judas Iscariot who was not a historical person. In this article it is my aim to make the further suggestion that many of the claims made of and for Jesus in the Gospels and 'The Acts of the Apostles' are dependent upon the Older Testament interpretative enterprise of St. Paul to be found in his highly developed Christology, and especially upon his understanding of Jesus' death as ordained by God as an atonement for humankind's sin.

I am quite aware that nineteenth and early twentieth century liberal Biblical scholars and theologians, guided, perhaps mainly, by German scholarship, made the claim which may be summarily stated as, "Paul took the straightforward religious and ethical teaching of Jesus and turned it into a highly complex theological and Christological manifesto relating to God's plan for humankind's salvation." This view came to be strongly opposed by the 'Neo-orthodox' mode of theological and Biblical scholarship represented, for example, by P. T. Forsyth in England and Karl Barth on the continent. Neo-orthodoxy, however, seems clearly to have had its day and its conclusions and assertions have for years been rigorously called into question by respected and responsible theologians and Biblical scholars world-wide. Certainly the claims of Crossan and Spong referred to above would have been anathema to both Forsyth and Barth. I do not know, however, of recent New Testament scholars in the Christian tradition who go as far as I aim to in this piece in assessing the influence of Paul on the composition of the Gospels. Hyam Maccoby in *The Mythmaker*[4] makes similar claims, though argued rather differently, and Robert Eisenman in his book *James the Brother of Jesus*, a somewhat repetitious *tour de force*, arrives at a similarly controversial view of Paul,[5] though again based on different interpretations of the evidence from those I am setting forth; it is a profound work, nonetheless.

Let me then make a bald (and bold?) introductory statement of the claims I wish to make about Paul as the first clear propagator of some of the major themes which the Gospel writers assert, and which most Christians and many others seem to take for granted as being current during Jesus' life and in the very early days after Jesus' crucifixion. In the rest of this essay I will provide the supporting evidence, reasons, and arguments which have led me to these conclusions. I will speak more fully about the role of 'speculation' in this study in my concluding paragraph; suffice it to say at this point that I am fully aware that many of my conclusions are speculative, *but* so are those of *every other* writer who seeks to unravel the problematic issues surrounding the life and death of Jesus and the beliefs and actions of his followers from the time of his crucifixion through the subsequent decades of the first century, C.E. This, I hope to show, is necessarily the case. I am going to make two major assertions, each of which has some important implications and 'rider' issues stemming from it. Firstly, Paul was the first one to declare unequivocally that Jesus *is* the Messiah, the Christ of God; that is to say, Christology, strictly speaking, began with Paul's interpretation of the significance of Jesus. Secondly, Paul was the first one to explain the thorny problem of a *crucified* Messiah, interpreting this as God's eternal plan to sacrifice God's Son to bear the world's sin and thus bring about an atonement, a reconciliation between God and humankind. The Cross as the focus of the *good news* of salvation was an insight first attributable to Paul, and resulted from his remarkable hermeneutical activity as he searched the Scriptures during the years following the Damascus road experience. It is these two issues and the assertions that stem from them, appearing frequently in the four gospels and the early chapters of Luke's second volume, *The Acts*, which I am claiming had their initial positive, formulated assertion in the mind and 'gospel' (as he himself calls it, *Romans* 2: 16) of Paul.

Now when I make the first assertion, namely, that Paul was the first person unequivocally to state that Jesus *is* the Christ, I am not meaning that merely in the sense of the literary, documentary appearance of the claim. That would be almost universally accepted. Nor am I for one moment claiming that the question of Jesus being the Christ was never mooted prior to Paul. Undoubtedly speculation around this issue occurred during Jesus' earthly ministry. The apocalyptic 'mood' of that time bred the expectation of 'one who should come' to bring 'this present age' to an end and inaugurate 'the age to come'. Subsequent to Jesus' execution, but not *immediately* following it, I aver, speculation about the significance of Jesus almost certainly continued. The compelling nature of Jesus' life and mission, his words and actions could not simply be forgotten. Such a speculation may well have led to a kind of incipient Christology such as suggested by the landmark, yet oft-neglected, essay by the late Bishop J. A. T. Robinson, entitled "The Most Primitive Christology of All."[6] The essay deals with the complex question as to the degree of credibility to be accorded to Luke's accounts in *Acts* of Peter's speeches as historically accurate. Robinson concludes that they cannot be understood simply as Luke's own viewpoint since they contain *conflicting* Christologies. At the conclusion of the speech in

Chapter 2 (v. 36), Peter asserts that "God has made him both *Lord* and *Christ*, this Jesus whom *you* (the Jews) crucified." In Chapter 3: 12-26, Peter concludes his speech with an urgent appeal to his listeners to repent, so that God "may *send* the Christ appointed for you, namely, Jesus, whom the heavens must retain until the time of the restoration of all things that God has spoken of through the mouth of the holy prophets since the beginning of this present age (*ap' aiōnos*, Gk.). Here, Jesus is seen as the one whom God *will send* as Messiah, or Christ, when 'this present Age' is at its end, to inaugurate 'the Age-to-Come', that being the mainstream Jewish Apocalyptic understanding of the function of Messiah. For Robinson, the 'most primitive Christology of all' is that Jesus 'will be' the Messiah, the Christ. And judging by the urgency of Peter's call to repentance, it seems that the coming of Jesus as Christ was believed to be in the near future. Bishop Krister Stendahl, at that time Morrison Professor of Biblical Studies at Harvard, apparently agreed with Robinson's suggestion, and on quite a few occasions in classes I attended there, spoke of the stages of developing thought by which the 'Will-be-ness' of Jesus' status as Christ became the 'Is-ness' that we find asserted in many places in the Gospels and the Epistles, and perhaps the 'Always-Has-Been-ness', depending on how John's Prologue, the first chapter of *Hebrews*, and the advanced Christologies of *Colossians* and *Ephesians* are interpreted.

Yet again, I am *not* asserting that 'Christianity' was 'invented' by Paul. The term 'Christianity' is susceptible of a variety of meanings. It has been maintained by some historians that as an organized 'religion' it really only began with the imperial proclamations of the Emperor Constantine. Broadly speaking, however, it has come to mean the faith held by followers of Jesus and there were thousands of those prior to Paul's Damascus road experience and its consequences. Paul's mandate from the Jerusalem High Priest to seek out and persecute followers of Jesus' 'Way' indicates some very vigorous and threatening activities on their part. I am concerned to establish the reasonableness of the speculation that the firm, unmistakeable assertions that Jesus was 'the Christ' and that his death on the Cross was a God-ordained sacrifice to make atonement for sin, both of which claims are made in the Gospels, though the latter claim is not, I believe, categorically stated in *Matthew*, were not an integral part of the message of the earliest followers of Jesus, but were incorporated into the Gospels by their writers/editors after they had been positively formulated by Paul. The earliest stratum of "Q"[7] consists of 'Wisdom' sayings, some of them in story form. What we commonly call 'The Sermon on the Mount' in Matthew contains a number of "Q" sayings paralleled in *Luke* 6: 20-49. "Q" material makes no mention of the title "Christ", nor any references to Jesus' death and resurrection. Yet this was the 'Gospel' of one of the early communities of Jesus' followers. I recall Dr. Stendahl once saying that if we wanted to know what was preached in the early 'church' in and around Jerusalem, The Beatitudes and the book of James may be as sure guides as we have available. While it is by no means certain that the book/epistle/homily of James was written by James the brother of Jesus, in fact, most probably not, its teaching and spirit are believed to reflect the beliefs and the mission of the church in which James served as pastor/bishop virtually until his death in the early 60s C.E. Even Paul acknowledges James' leadership, though somewhat grudgingly, methinks, if I read parts of the *Galatians* letter aright. 'Jesus Christ' (and not '*the* Christ') appears only twice in the letter, and even then is thought perhaps to be a later 'conforming' addition. No mention is made of Jesus' Cross and Resurrection. These facts I believe to be significant, though one cannot build a decisive case upon them.

We need to acknowledge the close connection between the ideas of Messiahship and resurrection from the dead. The German Dominican priest/Biblical scholar Joachim Becker has made a compelling case in his book, *Messianic Expectation in the Old Testament*.[8] He concludes that there is *no* 'Messianic Expectation' in the Hebrew Scriptures in the sense that such an expectation was strongly current in Jesus' day. The term '*the* Messiah' (*ha moshiach*) as pointing to 'one coming' does not occur in Scripture. 'The Lord's Anointed', ('the Messiah of Yahweh', 'the Christ of God') is frequently found, but it refers almost always to the kings of Judah and Israel, all of whom were Messiahs. They were also titled 'Son of God' (see *2 Samuel* 7: 14, and *Psalm* 2:

7), which is worth noting with respect to the use of that title for Jesus in the Christian Scriptures. The idea of a heaven-sent Messiah at the end of the present age is an apocalyptic notion which developed during the intertestamental period and was an issue of lively debate at the time of Jesus. It was accompanied by the expectation of the general resurrection of all the past faithful. This doctrine addressed the issue of theodicy, the justice of God, and God's reliability to fulfil promises made to the patriarchs. If God's 'New Age' would be established, when 'swords would be beaten into ploughshares and pruning hooks would replace spears', when 'the lion would lie down with the lamb', and 'the earth would be filled with the knowledge of God as the waters covered the sea,' and other visions of such prophets as Isaiah and Micah, then it would be unjust if all past yearners for this great day were to miss out on its arrival. Their bodies would be resurrected and they would share in the life of 'the Age to Come'. Any talk of Jesus' resurrection was posited on the belief of the 'general Resurrection'. Even Paul asserts this. In *1 Cor.* 15: 12 & 13, he asks, "How is it that some among you say there is no resurrection of the dead? If there is no resurrection of the dead, then Christ has not been raised!'

Krister Stendahl once said (in class) that if Peter had announced that God has raised Jesus, then almost every synagogue-attending Jew in the audience would have thought or said, "Then the general resurrection must have begun!' For Paul, the end of 'this age' is already present, and at the time of his writing the Thessalonian letters and a few years later the Corinthian letters, he is eagerly awaiting its dénouement, the general resurrection of the dead, an event he strongly believes in. It had begun with Jesus' resurrection. Crossan states, "It never occurs to Paul that Jesus' resurrection might be a special unique privilege given to him because he is Messiah."[9] But the converse must have been true for Paul, namely, that because he had spoken in a vision with the *living* Jesus *who had been dead*, Jesus must have been resurrected (not literally, physically) and by beginning the general resurrection, thus ending this age and inaugurating the 'age-to-come', Jesus must be the Christ, for that was one of the major views of the role of the coming heaven-sent Messiah. The visions of the risen Jesus are, in Paul's view, 'visions of a dead man who begins the general resurrection."[10] I agree, and this establishes Paul's claim that Jesus is the Christ, or as he puts it in *Romans* 1: 4: "... designated Son of God, by the resurrection of the dead."

But what of Jesus' followers prior to Paul? Had they already come to the same conclusions as Paul? We must honestly say that we have absolutely *no* documentary or other clear, certain evidence as to what beliefs about Jesus were held by his erstwhile followers in the remaining 30s after his death, nor in the 40s C.E. in and around Jerusalem where James' episcopy held sway, nor in Samaria. It appears from the story of Stephen in *Acts* 6 & 7, judging by the content and thrust of his long speech, that Stephen probably had Samaritan leanings, the speech being strongly Moseocentric. Not once does he refer to Jesus as the Christ, but hinted that he was 'the prophet like unto me whom God will raise up from among your brethren,' whom Moses had foretold (*Acts* 7: 37). While the story does have Jesus exalted at God's right hand, there is noticeably no reference to his resurrection. We have already noted that in the early "Q" 'Gospel' and in the book of James there is nothing strictly about the Messiahship of Jesus, of his resurrection, or of his death as an atonement. Returning now to the question of the situation the followers of Jesus found themselves in after his execution, I offer the opinion that no matter what speculations may have been abroad during his ministry as to his Messiahship, all such thinking ended with his crucifixion. The idea of God's Messiah being put to a criminal's death would have been unthinkable to the minds of mainstream, pious Jews waiting for a God-sent deliverer.

Luke's Emmaus Road story is, I believe, a vignette of the faith-journey of the companions of Jesus, written, we should note, by Paul's fellow-traveller, Luke. At the outset the two journeying home are bewildered for they "had hoped that Jesus was to be the one who would redeem Israel" (*Luke* 24: 21). I have no doubt that Jesus' followers who were in and around Jerusalem at the time of the crucifixion were bewildered and utterly down-hearted. That mood must have lasted some considerable time, unless we take the story of the Resurrection as told in the Gospels at face value. Yet I believe the period of grieving would not have gone on indefinitely. They'd recall Jesus' words and his commission to his followers to go into the villages and hamlets and announce not that the Kingdom of God was imminent, but that it was *present* and all who wished could share in a just community where all were equal. This mission need not be stopped by Jesus' death since Jesus did not claim to be the mediator or bearer of that kingdom.

To quote Crossan again: "Jesus ... does not say 'I bring the kingdom' or that he or anyone else has a monopoly or franchise on it. Rather he announces that it's permanently available to anyone and everyone, everywhere ... Jesus essentially says, "The kingdom is here, *you don't even need me.*"[11] (italics mine) Many, probably most, of Jesus' followers were not present at the time of his death and may not have heard of it until weeks later.

In a question and answer session at a seminar on 'Jesus' held at the University of Winnipeg, and at which Dr. Crossan was present, a question was raised about the itinerant couples going amongst the villages to announce the kingdom's presence, and amongst other things Dr. Crossan mentioned that if, after Jesus' death, someone had met a couple in a southern Galilee hamlet actively engaged in the work Jesus had sent them to do, and had informed them that Jesus had been executed, he imagined that they may well have replied, "Oh, we're very saddened to hear it; but our work must still go on," or words to that effect. The point of all this is to emphasize that some lively mission work continued after Jesus' death, but it wasn't concerned with proclaiming Jesus as Christ, nor is there any necessity to suppose the beginning of the general resurrection was any part of the message. Crossan insisted that Jesus did *not* send the paired disciples out in *his* name, but to announce the actual presence of God's kingdom and the availability to all of its egalitarian communal life.

A fact that is worth serious reflection is that many, if not most, scholars in the mainstream of New Testament study are hesitant to say unequivocally that Jesus declared himself to be the Christ. All the Gospels and much of the early part of *Acts* use that title: but *that* is the central question of this paper. Matthew has Peter declare "Thou art the Christ," and has Jesus roundly approving of Peter's confession: "Blessed are you, Simon bar Jonas, for flesh and blood has not revealed this to you but my Father in heaven" (*Matt.* 16: 16 & 17). By the time Matthew's Gospel came into something like its present form, the writer/editor is certain of Jesus' Messiahship. He also asserts that the general resurrection *did actually occur* at the crucifixion/resurrection time, thus *confirming* the expectations of the Messiah's coming, (*Matt.* 27: 52 & 53), but no other Gospel writer will touch that! It is easy to say that Matthew is speaking metaphorically, but I think not! Peter's confession in the Marcan parallel passage (*Mark* 8: 29ff.) brings no kind word of approval from Jesus but the stern statement, "Tell no one that concerning me!' This has been thought of, since the work of W. Wrede, as 'the Messianic secret', a phrase much used, often by those who have not read Wrede's explication of the words. It is therefore thought of as Jesus' own mind and his desire not to have his Messiahship broadcast. Wrede's point was that these words were a Marcan insertion to explain the discrepancy between the clear, open acclamation of Jesus as the Christ by the time Paul's epistles were written, that is, by the middle of the first century C.E., and the comparative lack of clear affirmation of his Messiahship by Jesus himself in his teaching and ministry. The words, "Tell no one about me," as a reply to Peter's "You are the Christ!", may very well mean "Don't you go saying that about me!" Further evidence of the historical Jesus' ambivalence as to Messiahship may be seen in his answers to the High Priest and to Pilate. When the High Priest said to Jesus, "Tell us whether you are the Christ," Jesus is recorded as answering, "Thou sayest," and to Pilate's question, "Are you the King of the Jews?" (a Messianic title), Jesus gave the same ambiguous answer, which may mean, "You've said it!" but could as probably mean, "That's what *you* say," a virtual denial. While the detailed reports of these two incidents are unlikely to be historically accurate, their occurrence in the Gospels does indicate a hesitation on the writers'/editors' part to have Jesus make clear claim to Messiahship, their assertions of such in other parts of their record notwithstanding.

If that considerable number of scholars who believe that Jesus did *not* himself claim to be the Christ, as well as many more who are at least doubtful of it, are *right*, then the erstwhile companions of Jesus, after a time of bewilderment and grieving, then returning to engage in the mission of announcing the presence of God's kingdom, would doubtless remember many of his sayings, for example, "Blessed are you poor", but they would *not* remember his claim to be the Christ, because Jesus had never made that claim. They had a working method of continuing to announce the 'good news' of the kingdom, introduced to them by Jesus but not *needing* Jesus for its practice or even its success. As cited above, "Jesus essentially said, 'The kingdom is here; you don't even need me.'" They likely felt the presence of their now dead Master as they went about the work Jesus had set them to do. The reality of the presence of persons who have died being experienced by the living as visions and not psychotic hallucinations is common enough even today,[12] and was probably accepted as a well-known phenomenon in Jesus' time. But what would have made them feel that Jesus' presence had anything to do with the general resurrection, in which they almost all certainly believed? I suspect it didn't remotely occur to them; why should it have? I conclude then that for years after his death, Jesus' message continued to be preached and to be as troublesome to the Roman authorities and many amongst the officialdom of the Jerusalem temple, since it inveighed against the unconscionable injustices practised against the peasant workers in southern Galilee by advocating an egalitarian kingdom of God. Maccoby states, "Scholars have not been able to deny that the Jerusalem Church, under the leadership of James, consisted of practising Jews, loyal to the Torah ...[as was Jesus].[13] These followers of 'the Way' were known not as Nazarenes, as often supposed, but as *Nazōraioi* (*Acts* 24: 5), (the Talmudic name for them being *notzerim*), from a Hebrew root meaning 'keepers' of the Law.[14] They had special concern for 'the poor' and were later nicknamed 'Ebionites', from the Hebrew *ebhyonim*, meaning 'poor ones'. The impression of unity between these and Paul "so sedulously cultivated by the author of *Acts* is a sham and there is much evidence, both in *Acts* itself and in Paul's Epistles, that there was serious conflict between the Pauline and the Jerusalem interpretations of Jesus' message."[15]

With respect to the problem of a crucified Messiah we find that Paul's Christology includes a strong soteriological or 'saviourhood' component. God put forward or offered up Jesus the Christ "as an expiation [for sin] by his blood" (*Romans* 3: 25). Jesus' blood shed on the Cross is seen as a God-ordained universal atonement replacing the need for the yearly sacrifice of *yom kippur*, the Day of Atonement (*Exodus* 30: 10; *Levit.* 23: 27). This theme runs throughout Paul's letters and to a much lesser extent it appears in the Gospels. It is also testified to in the so-called Epistles of Peter. Luke has the risen Christ say on the road to Emmaus, "*Ought not* the Christ to have suffered," seemingly indicating that the Cross was part of God's eternal plan. John understands Jesus' being 'lifted up' on the Cross as God's way of drawing all to Godself (*John* 3: 14; 12: 32). He has Jesus say that unless we drink his blood we will have no life in us (*John* 6: 53). This reflects Paul's words to the Corinthians: "The cup of blessing which we bless, is it not a participation in the blood of Christ?" (*1 Cor.* 10: 16), and his words about the institution of the 'Lord's Supper' or Eucharist, which, mark you well, Paul claims to have received directly from Jesus, presumably in a vision, where he states, "This cup is the new covenant in my blood; do this as often as you drink it, in remembrance of me" (*1 Cor.* 11: 25). Drinking blood, forbidden by the Torah, would surely have been utterly repugnant to Jesus and his Galilean followers and it is almost unthinkable that he would have asked them at any of their shared, open-table, fellowship meals to drink his blood, even if intended symbolically. Paul seems to have been given a number of visions by which he claims his authority. He speaks forcibly of this authority in *Galatians*, Chapter 1: "... the gospel which I preach(ed) is not a human gospel. For I did not receive it from any human source, nor was I taught it, but it came by a revelation of Jesus Christ" (vv.11 and 12). As for being guided by Jesus' followers in Jerusalem, he speaks disparagingly of them. Those so-called pillars of the movement who 'were reputed to be something, though what they were makes no difference to me!' They, Paul repeats for emphasis, 'added nothing to me!' (2: 6). So much for the insistence of a major scholar in this field of enquiry, Professor Helmut Koester of Harvard, that "... As far as the churches of Judea and Jerusalem are concerned, the traditions preserved in the Pauline Corpus are probably a better witness for their praxis than the sayings and narratives preserved in the Synoptic tradition."[16] In addition to the eucharistic meal, Koester believes the death/resurrection story, as Paul sets it out in *1 Corinthians* 15: 1-11, has been derived by Paul from the tradition of the Judean and Jerusalem church communities.[17] Paul writes that he had 'handed on' to the Corinthians that which he had 'in turn' *received*, namely "that *Christ died for our sins* in accordance with the scriptures ... that he was *raised on the third day* in accordance with the scriptures ... that he appeared first to Cephas, then to the twelve, then to more than 500 persons, then to James, then to all the apostles." Paul does *not* say in this passage, however, that he received this information from other church officials and it may well have come to him in a further visionary revelation. There are three things at least in this piece of Paul's correspondence which make me reluctant to attribute its details to the earlier Judean tradition: Paul's use of 'Christ' and not 'Jesus' whose death for sins was predicted in the Scriptures; Christ's resurrection 'on the third day' having been predicted in the Scriptures; and then the order of the appearances of the 'risen Christ' which differs from all other accounts, with James, Jesus' brother and leader of the Jerusalem community, last on the list of his 'received' tradition! While I've little doubt, as stated above, that some of Jesus' close followers experienced the sense of his presence after he had been executed, I doubt that they preceded Paul in finding a soteriological meaning for his crucifixion in their Scriptures. Nor, I believe, were those experiences of Jesus' presence likely to have been had just two days after his death. "On the third day" was God's revealed "new life giving" symbolic time-table according to the prophet *Hosea* (6: 1 & 2), a detail which smacks of Paul's ingenious midrashic interpretations.

John Dominic Crossan, from whose recent monumental study, *The Birth of Christianity*, I have taken the above citations of Koester's work, does not seem to be wholly convinced that Paul knew a traditional *story* of the death and resurrection of Jesus, but suggests that if Paul did it may have been from an early version of the non-canonical *Gospel of Peter*, sections of which have been called by Crossan, the 'Cross Gospel'.[18] I speculate that it was very highly *improbable* that Paul had access to such a document, even if it were in existence by the 50s C.E. It is not at all impossible that Paul had heard of Jesus while living in the precincts of Jerusalem; he may have even heard Jesus speak, or at least have known the tenor of his message and mission. I believe that there must have been some deep inner conflict between Paul's mandated task to persecute "those of the 'Way'" and some deep respect he held for that 'Way'. Paul blacked out on his journey and had the vision of Jesus, who spoke to him. I reiterate again that *that* experience led to his formulation of his 'gospel' as set out above. The former companions of Jesus would have interpreted his death as the almost expected outcome of Jesus' message which exposed without compromise the rank injustices practised against the poor Jewish peasants in southern Galilee's agrarian economy, not to mention its stinging critique of the hypocritical stance of some religious leaders. They may well have thought about what it might mean *for them* to be proclaiming the same 'good news' of God's kingdom, an egalitarian society, with open table-fellowship and open healing of society's hurts and injustices. I don't believe they held any deep theological or Christological thoughts or theories about Jesus' death, nor of any imminent general resurrection. Nearly half a century ago, a prominent Australian New Testament scholar, the late Revd Dr. W. Frank Hambly, said in a classroom lecture, "If someone had met a group of Jesus' disciples six months after the crucifixion and had said to them, 'Your Scriptures say, *Cursed be every one who is hanged on a tree*' (*Deut.* 21: 23), they would not have had any idea how to answer."[19] Paul, however, knows exactly how to respond! He argues, "Christ redeemed us from the curse of the law, *having become a curse for us*" (*Gal.* 3: 13). A fantastic piece of interpretation!

Thus far I have shown from the reliable documentary evidence of letters almost universally accepted as authored by Paul, that his 'gospel' asserted (a) that Jesus *is* 'the Christ'; (b) that the general resurrection had already begun; and that Jesus' death was a God-ordained 'transaction' whereby human sin has been atoned for. I have also *speculated*, on what I believe to be strong grounds, that such doctrines were not part of the message of the earliest followers of Jesus. The issue needing still to be addressed is this: "How did these teachings come to be proclaimed in the canonical gospels as an assured part of the message of the historical Jesus?" Since the composition of all these gospels – with perhaps the exception of sections taken from the earliest stratum of the 'sayings-source' "Q" – took place *after* Paul's ingenious formulation of these doctrines, I do not find the answer to the above question difficult to understand. Paul claims in *Galatians*, a letter which contains some rather disparaging, if not hostile, references to Peter and James, that he met with James, Peter, and John at what we non-conformists often refer to as 'The Jerusalem Church Meeting'(!) (*Acts* 15), where, after he had explained the revelatory mandate he had been given by 'the Lord' to preach among the Gentiles, these three 'pillars of the Jerusalem Church', who, Paul had just finished writing, "added nothing to me" yet gave him their blessing on his Gentile mission and offered him 'the right hand of fellowship' (*Gal.* 2: 9).

The genius of Paul is that he universalized what was a comparatively small provincial 'Jesus Movement'; and the significance of the 'Jesus event', understood in the terms of Paul's 'gospel', began to spread successfully throughout the Hellenized/Roman world, both Eastern and Western Christianity being the heirs of this 'gospel'. But at what cost? Paul, the mission strategist, makes sure not to fall foul of Roman authority as much as he could, telling his converts to "be subject to the governing (Roman) authorities," which, he states, "have been instituted by God" (*Romans* 13: 1). In his earliest letters to the Thessalonians he states that it was the Jews "who killed our Lord Jesus" (*1 Thess.* 2: 14 & 15), thus exonerating the Romans of the crime, a stance, from a historical point of view, now strongly refuted.[20] I speculate that the small Jerusalem-centred group of Jesus' followers was beginning to lose some of its missionary impact through persecution and a dwindling in numbers by the late 40s C.E., and may have found fresh impetus, on the part of *some* of its leaders, in Paul's Scripturally derived interpretation of Jesus' life, death and resurrection and its successful flourishing in distant cities of the Roman Empire. I believe that Paul was the major mind behind both the passages in Hebrew prophecy being understood as fulfilled in Jesus' life and death, and the Scriptural interpretations of the Abraham story, the words of *Habakkuk* 2: 4, and the Suffering Servant passages in *Isaiah* 52: 13ff., and Ch. 53, which form the basis of his own 'gospel'. I believe that Peter and John at least came to embrace Paul's wider, universally applicable and preachable message as the way for the future. The Gospel attributed to the 'School of John' and the letters attributed to Peter, which, though not written by Peter himself, must have reflected the later teaching of the Petrine 'circle', clearly echo Paul's cardinal emphases as set out earlier in this paper. I very much doubt, however, if James, Jesus' brother, ever wholeheartedly accepted Paul's views, and if the letter of James reflects the teaching of the Jerusalem and Judean 'churches', there is both evidence of debate on the 'faith/works' issue, but little 'Christic' emphasis, and *no* 'atonement through Jesus' death' proclamation. This group seems to have continued through sects such as the Ebionites, who revered James, thought of Jesus as a good man, even perhaps a Messiah in the line of Moses who was considered God's 'Anointed' *par excellence*, but *not* in the sense of what Joachim Becker, cited earlier, called 'real Messianism', and coming of a heaven-sent Deliverer.[21] They followed the commandments of the Torah and sought to do what God required, perhaps best expressed as "to do justice, to love kindness and to walk humbly with God" (*Micah* 6: 8). In this, I believe they remained faithful to the 'way' of Jesus, of his brother James, and the earliest communities of Jesus' companions.

I have called this piece 'A Speculation *Revisited*' because much of what I have written and argued for was a lively issue in the nineteenth century represented in the works of scholars such as F. C. Baur of Tübingen. The reader will have noted that I have quite often cited John Dominic Crossan in ways that have been advantageous to my argument. His recent masterly, nay, magisterial work, *The Birth of Christianity*,[22] the erudite, detailed scholarship undergirding the which, I stand in awe of, has been written (not purposely or specifically, of course,) to show how wrongheaded the speculations of this paper are! I have found the book enormously stimulating, informative, and indeed, helpful ... yet, much of it is speculation, very strongly supported and well argued, but speculation nonetheless. Much of the detailed support for some of his major conclusions depends on sources that are essentially irrelevant to my case since they are written after what amounts in this paper to the conversion of some of the major leaders of the primitive Jerusalem community to Paul's views. Some of the references to the 'Recognitions' in the Pseudo-Clementine tales seem to me positively to support my view, but even so such writings are no more historically reliable than *Acts*. It is of little use even to quote a writer like Josephus in search of information about Jesus' followers in the 30s and early 40s C.E. Josephus would only have been a teenager (precocious, by repute) when Paul wrote the Corinthian letters and, as I have suggested, from that time on much of what would have been seen, heard of, or written about primitive 'Christianity', was already coloured by Paul's ever-widening influence. The canonical Gospels were no exception; their Christological, soteriological, and apocalyptic viewpoints allegedly attributed to Jesus have their source in Paul's fertile mind. So I speculate. I rest my case.

ENDNOTES

Chapter 1:

[1] Ian MacLaren: *Beside the Bonnie Brier Bush* (London: Hodder & Stoughton, first edition 1894), p. 85.
[2] Martin Buber: *Two Types of Faith*, p. 12, cited in Earl K. Holt, III. "Martin Buber and Jesus and Us", *The Unitarian Universalist Christian*, Vol. 43, No. 1, pp. 21 & 22.
[3] Cited in class at Boston University School of Theology (1961) by Professor Edwin Prince Booth, a Church historian and author of the book *Martin Luther: Oak of Saxony* (Nashville: Abingdon Press, 1965).
[4] Marcus Borg: "What Did Jesus Know?", *Biblical Review*, Dec. 1995, pp. 19 & 48.
[5] Formerly Dean of the Divinity School, Harvard University, later Bishop of Stockholm, and even later, Distinguished Professor at Brandeis University, Dr. Stendahl is one of the major experts on Jewish-Christian relations.

Chapter 2:

[1] From *The Hymnal of the Moravian Church* (1969), No. 339.
[2] See, for example, *Psalm* 103: vv. 3 & 12; *Isaiah* 55: 7.
[3] A past participle from the Hebrew verb 'to seek or search'. When Jesus said, "Ye search the Scriptures ..." he would have used that Semitic verb. There is a multiple-volume body of published ancient *midrashim* where verse after verse of the Torah is intricately explained often in relation to other passages. For example, "In the beginning ..." (Hebrew *bereshith*) is explained in the light of a passage in *Proverbs* 8: 22, where Wisdom calls herself 'the beginning (Initiator?) of God's way or work'; 'by means of Wisdom, God created the heavens and the earth.' The New Testament is fraught with *midrashim* interpreting events in the life and words of Jesus in the light of Old Testament passages and *vice versa*.
[4] See André Schwarz-Bart: *The Last of the Just* (New York: Athenaeum, 1973, p. 57; also London: Vintage Classics, 2001). This is a book I wish all Christians would read!

Chapter 3:

[1] *The Hibbert Journal*, Vol. 49, Jan. 1951, pp. 128-136 (see Ch. 4, n.[7]).
[2] Ryan Asmussen: "The Persistence of Memory: An Interview with Paula Fredriksen", *Focus*, Spring 2003 (Boston School of Theology), p.10.
[3] For example, every king of Israel or Judah was 'the anointed *of Yahweh*', and the prophet Isaiah (Deutero or Trito) stated that Yahweh's Spirit had *anointed* him to preach good news ... (*Isaiah* 61: 1 & 2).
[4] Joachim Becker: *Messianic Expectation in the Old Testament* (Philadelphia, Pennsylvania: Fortress Press, 1980), pp. 87 & 93.

ENDNOTES

⁵ *Ibid.*
⁶ Cited in Richard N. Soulen: "Behind Apocalyptic", *Religion in Life*, Vol. 43, No. 1, pp. 100ff.
⁷ See Albert Schweitzer: *The Quest of the Historical Jesus* (London: A. & C. Black, 1910), pp. 357-362, and pp. 385-390; also published by John Hopkins Press, 1998. I add here that Schweitzer's "apocalyptic" Jesus was a dogmatically driven revolutionary, though not necessarily militaristic, even if such reported sayings as "I am come not to bring peace but a sword" seem to lean in that direction (see *Matthew* 10: 34 and *Luke* 22: 36). I believe Schweitzer is correct about the early ministry of Jesus but I believe that when the apocalyptic preacher, John the Baptist, was slain and God made no intervention, Jesus forswore apocalypticism and preached the here and now *presence* of the Kin(g)dom of God. It is this later post-apocalyptic Jesus whom I seek to follow and for whom I 'speak this good word'.
⁸ *Ibid.* pp. 368 and 369.
⁹ *Ibid.* pp. 369 and 397.
¹⁰ *Ibid.* p. 401.
¹¹ J. A. T. Robinson: "The Most Primitive Christology of All", *The Journal of Theological Studies*, New Series, Vol. VII, 1956, pp. 177-189.
¹² *Ibid.* pp. 181-2, italics mine.
¹³ See T. F. Glasson: *The Second Advent: The Development of a Doctrine* (London: Epworth Press, 1963), and J. A. T. Robinson, *Jesus and His Coming* (London: SCM Press, 1957).
¹⁴ In a conversation with Robert Maddox at Harvard Divinity School in 1962. Also see p. 94 regarding W. Wrede's so-called 'Messianic secret'.

Chapter 4:

¹ R. N. Soulen: "Behind Apocalyptic", *Religion in Life*, Vol. 43, No. 1, pp. 100ff.
² *Acts* 3: 19-21.
³ The oft-cited passage from 'The Fourth Book of Ezra' (II Esdras), Ch. 7 was written even after the publication of many of the New Testament documents and reflects Christian influence.
⁴ *The Birth of Christianity* (San Francisco: HarperCollins, 1998), p. xix.
⁵ *Ibid.*
⁶ Paula Fredriksen: "My Quest for the Historical Jesus", *Bostonia*, Summer 1999, No. 2, pp. 87-90.
⁷ See W. R. Inge: "Liberal Christianity", *The Hibbert Journal*, Vol. 49, Jan. 1951, p. 130f.
⁸ Albert Schweitzer, *The Quest of the Historical Jesus, op. cit.*, p. 399.
⁹ See note 7.
¹⁰ I am sure this brief quotation is accurate but cannot find its documentary source. Borg, however, says essentially the same thing in his piece, "Faith and Scholarship", *Biblical Review*, August 1993, pp. 9 and 54.

Chapter 5:

[1] William Herzog: *Parables As Subversive Speech: Jesus as Pedagogue of the Oppressed* (Louisville, Kentucky: Westminster/John Knox Press, 1994).
[2] *Ibid.* p. 7.
[3] *Ibid.* pp. 150-168.
[4] E.g., *Isaiah* 1: 17 and 23; *Jeremiah* 22: 3; *Ezekiel* 22: 7; and *Zechariah* 7: 10.
[5] Marcus Borg: "What Did Jesus Know?", *Biblical Review*, Dec. 1995, pp. 19 and 48.

Chapter 6:

[1] See the appraisal ("blurb") on the back cover of John Dominic Crossan's *The Birth of Christianity* (San Francisco: HarperCollins, 1998).
[2] See the reference in Robert Eisenman, *James the Brother of Jesus* (New York: Viking, 1996), p. 529.
[3] *Acts* 7: 37, citing *Deuteronomy* 18: 15 and 18.
[4] J. A. T. Robinson: "The Most Primitive Christology of All?", *The Journal of Theological Studies*, New Series, Vol. 7 (1956), pp. 177-189.
[5] See Paul Trudinger: "The Priority of *2 Thessalonians* Revisited," *The Downside Review*, Vol. 113 (Jan. 1995), pp. 31-35.
[6] See M. Wise, M. Abegg, Jr., and E. Cook: *The Dead Sea Scrolls: A New Translation* (San Francisco: HarperCollins, 1996), p. 49, for the citing of Solomon Schechter's discovery.
[7] *Ibid.* p. 50. See also Robert Eisenman, *op. cit.*, pp. 82 & 83 and 268.
[8] See Robert Eisenman, *op. cit.*, pp. 735-744. Eisenman has suggested that the subversive 'insider' adversary spoken of in the Habbakuk *Pesher* as the 'spouter of lies' might well be Paul who beguiled some members of the Qumran community with his interpretation of the Scriptures as applying to Jesus. They seceded from the community when 'the spouter of lies' was expelled according to the Habbakuk *Pesher*. Eisenman points out how Paul in a number of places insists that he is not a liar: "I speak the truth; I lie not." (See *Romans* 9: 1; *Galatians* 1: 20; *2 Corinthians* 11: 31)
[9] André Schwarz-Bart: *The Last of the Just* (New York: Athenaeum, 1973), pp. 56 & 57.
[10] See *1 Peter* 1: 18 & 19; 3: 18; *John* 1: 29; 3: 14-17; *1 John* 2: 1 & 2; *Revelation* 13: 8.
[11] "The Historical Jesus: An Interview with John Dominic Crossan", *The Christian Century*, December 18–25, 1991, p. 1202.
[12] *Luke* 10: 17.
[13] See details in Appendix 'B', and Paul Trudinger: "The Gospels as Pauline Christology Historicized", *Faith and Freedom*, Vol. 54, Part 1, pp. 34-45.

Chapter 7:

[1] Michael Morwood: *Is Jesus God?* (Melbourne: Spectrum Publications, 2001).

ENDNOTES

See especially p. 118, and his words "Jesus affirms our connectedness to God and sets us free from fear."
[2] See the hymn-text "God the Father, Be Thou Near," stanza 4, line 2, no. 952 in *The Methodist Hymn Book* (London, 1933, eighth edition, 1962), p. 850.
[3] This is a phrase used often by Quaker, Paul Lacey, of Earlham College, Indiana, U.S.A., in his book *Education and the Inward Teacher*, as cited by W. N. Oats, *Values Education* (Hobart: The Friends' School, 1995), p. 84.
[4] See A. R. Peacocke: *Evolution: The Disguised Friend of Faith?* (Conshohocken, Pennsylvania: Templeton Foundation Press, 2005). This is a book of previously published essays. Also *The Palace of Glory: God's World and Science* (Adelaide, South Australia: ATF Press, 2005), pp. 2-18. This is a book of lectures recently given in China.
[5] "Orthodoxy", *The British Weekly*, Feb. 12, 1959, p. 4.

Chapter 8:

[1] Elizabeth Goudge: *The Scent of Water* (New York: Coward-McCann, Inc., 1963) p.115.

Appendix 'A':

[1] Ronald A. Knox (transl.): *The Old Testament, Vol. II* (London: Burns Oates & Washbourne, Ltd., 1949), pp. 760-61.
[2] Samuel Terrien, *Job* in *The Interpreter's Bible, Vol. III* (New York: Abingdon Press, 1954), p. 1051.
[3] W. A. Irwin, *Job* in *Peake's Commentary on the Bible*, ed. M. Black and H. H. Rowley, (London and New York: Routledge, 1962-1997) p. 399.
[4] Archibald MacLeish: *J.B. – A Play in Verse*, (Boston: The Houghton Mifflin Company, 1958).
[5] H. McKeating: "The Central Issue of the Book of Job", *The Expository Times*, Vol. 82, 1971, pp. 244-247. McKeating makes no reference to *Job* 19: 25 & 26 in support of his conclusion.
[6] Professor Norman Habel: *The Book of Job* – The Old Testament Library (London: SCM Press, 1982), p. 583.
[7] I am in agreement with those who claim that the story originally ended at Chapter 42: 9. The next seven verses in which Job's fortunes are restored (in spades) seem to have been added by a 'happy ending' advocate of Deuteronomistic ethics: 'the righteous shall prosper'. These verses do not support our understanding of the book's purpose; in many ways they spoil the story.
[8] Irwin, *loc. cit.*
[9] United Bible Societies, *Good News Bible: Today's English Version*, 1976-1985.

Appendix 'B':

[1] J. D. Crossan: *Who Killed Jesus?* (San Francisco, HarperCollins, 1995), p. 1.

[2] J. S. Spong: *Liberating the Gospels* (San Francisco: HarperCollins, 1997), pp. 257-276.
[3] Audio tape lent to me by a Lutheran pastor who attended the Public Lecture in Vancouver, July 2, 1996.
[4] H. Maccoby: *The Mythmaker: Paul and the Invention of Christianity*, (New York: Barnes & Noble, 1986; London: Weidenfeld & Nicolson, 1986).
[5] R. Eisenman: *James the Brother of Jesus*, (New York: Viking Penguin, 1997), pp. 51-2, 527-9, 648-51, 703-5, 875-880, 926-7, 939, *et passim*.
[6] J. A. T. Robinson: "The Most Primitive Christology of All?" (Oxford: *The Journal of Theological Studies*, New Series VII, 1956), p. 177-189.
[7] See B. L. Mack: *The Lost Gospel: The Book of "Q" and Christian Origins* (San Francisco: HarperCollins, 1993); and J. Kloppenborg: *The Formation of "Q"* (Philadelphia: Fortress Press, 1987).
[8] J. Becker, OP: *Messianic Expectation in the Old Testament* (Philadelphia: Fortress Press, 1980), pp. 87 and 93.
[9] J. D. Crossan: *The Birth of Christianity*, p. xix.
[10] J. D. Crossan, *ibid*.
[11] "The Historical Jesus: An Interview with John Dominic Crossan", *The Christian Century*, December 18–25, 1991, p. 1202.
[12] See the evidence put forward in J. D. Crossan's *Birth of Christianity*, noted above, xvi and xvii.
[13] H. Maccoby, *op. cit.*, p. 172.
[14] R. Eisenman, *op.cit.*, pp. 227-8; 242-5.
[15] H. Maccoby, *op.cit., ibid.*
[16] H. Koester, "Jesus' Presence in the Early Church," *Cristianesimo nella Storia*, Vol. 15: pp. 541-557, (1994), cited in J. D. Crossan's *The Birth of Christianity*, p. 423.
[17] H. Koester, *op.cit.*, again cited in Crossan's *The Birth of Christianity*, pp. 546-7.
[18] J. D. Crossan: *The Birth of Christianity*, p. 548.
[19] Dr. Frank Hambly served for a term as President-General of the Methodist Church of Australia. He was Master of Lincoln College, University of Adelaide. This lecture was delivered in 1956. Though an outstanding imaginative Biblical scholar, he published very little, unfortunately.
[20] This is the subject of J. D. Crossan's book, *Who Killed Jesus?* noted above.[1]
[21] J. Becker, *op. cit.*, states, "It is on the threshold of the New Testament that we encounter a 'Real Messianism'", p. 87.
[22] We have noted that Robert Funk, Chair of 'The Jesus Seminar', wrote on the back-cover that "the stunning hypothesis of this book is that Christianity arose out of the interaction of the historical Jesus and his first companions. It was not invented by Paul." I commend the book to readers interested in this matter. I must admit that often during my reading of it, I felt like Agrippa listening to Paul: "Almost persuaded!" The operative word in that phrase is *almost!*

Index

OF PERSONS CITED IN THE TEXT, APPENDICES AND ENDNOTES

Abegg, M. 104
Asmussen, R. 102

Bach, J. S. 12
Barth, Karl 17, 78, 87f
Baur, F. C. 100
Becker, J. 26f., 90, 100, 102, 106
Bodycomb, John iv, 14, 69
Bodycomb, Mavis iv, 14
Booth, E. P. 102
Borg, M. 10, 44f., 50, 102, 103, 104
Buber, Martin 8, 102

Carr, P. 48, 49
Cook, E. 104
Crossan, J. D. 14, 15, 23, 36f., 38f., 54, 60, 73f., 86, 87, 87, 91, 93f., 97, 98f., 100, 104f., 105, 106f

Davies, Paul 63f., 65
Dawkins, Richard 63, 71
Dodd, C. H. 31

Eisenman, Robert 87, 104f., 106f

Finnis, J. 67

Forsyth, P. T. 87f
Fox, George 65
Fredriksen, Paula 25, 38, 102, 103
Funk, Robert 54, 104, 106

Gandhi, Mahatma 8
Glasson, T. F. 103
Goudge, E. 74, 105
Graham, Billy 78

Habel, N. 84, 105
Hambly, W. F. 98, 106
Handel, G. F. 19, 43, 82, 85
Herzog, W. 45, 46, 48f., 104

Inge, W. R. 24, 33, 43, 103
Irwin, W. A. 83, 85, 105f

Jones, E. Stanley 8

Kaesemann, E. 27
Kirke 75
Kloppenborg, J. 106
Knox, R. (Msgr) 82, 105
Koester, H. 96, 97f., 106f
Kushner, Rabbi Harold 14

Lacey, P. 51, 74, 105
Lewis, C. S. 42

Luther, Martin 9, 102

Maccoby, H. 87, 95, 106f
Mack, B. L. 106
MacLaren, Ian 7, 102
MacLeish, A. 84, 105
Maddox, R. 32, 103
McKeating, H. 84, 105
Micklem, N. 72
Moffatt, J. 83
Morwood, M. 62, 104

Oats, W. N. 105

Peacocke, A. R. 69-71, 105

Rawson, G. 18, 66, 105
Robinson, J. A. T. 30f., 31, 55, 88, 89, 103, 104, 106

Schechter, Solomon 57, 104
Schwarz-Bart, André 59, 102, 104
Schweitzer, Albert iv, 28f., 29f., 42, 44f., 103f
Simon, Marcel 55
Soulen, R. N. 103f
Spong, J. S. 86, 87, 106
Stendahl, K. 13, 30, 32, 55, 89, 90, 91, 102

Terrien, S. 82, 105
Tillich, P. 22, 66, 80
Trudinger, P. 104f

Wise, M. 104
Wrede, W. 94f., 103

Yahgan, Murat 8